THE WRITER'S BLOCK MYTH

A Guide to Get Past Stuck &
Experience Lasting Creative Freedom

Heloise Jones

LIFESTYLE
ENTREPRENEURS
P R E S S

All rights reserved.

Copyright © 2016 by Heloise Jones
www.HeloiseJones.com

No part of this book may be reproduced or transmitted in any form or any means, electronic or mechanical, including photocopying, recording, or by any information storage or retrieval system, without permission in writing from the Publisher.

Copyright Notice

Publisher: Jesse Krieger
Write to Jesse@JesseKrieger.com if you are interested in publishing through Lifestyle Entrepreneurs Press.

Publications or foreign rights acquisitions of our catalogue books.
Learn More: www.LifestyleEntrepreneursPress.com

Any unauthorized use, sharing, reproduction or distribution of these materials by any means, electronic, mechanical or otherwise is strictly prohibited. No portion of these materials may be reproduced in any manner whatsoever, without the express written consent of the publisher.

ISBN: 978-1-946697-04-2

Dedicated to the courageous writers, artists, and thinkers charting their course, making a map only they can make, willing to live their best creative life.

TABLE OF CONTENTS

The Writer's Block Myth - Introduction 1

The Inner Game
7 Keys to Set You Free to Write 17

#1 Pay Attention to the Evidence Journal 22

#2 Let Go of Dead-End Distractions, and Do What Answers Yes 26

#3 Trust the Permeable Boundaries of the Creative Process 30

Get Curious 31

Let Go of Expectations 34

#4 Connection is Alchemical. Writing is Connection 40

#5 Rejection Happens, so Cheer the Triumphs 43

The Inner Critic, A Twisted Friend 48

Perfectionism, The Inner Critic's Buddy 48

Change the Word *Sacrifice* to *Choice* 50

#6 You Define Success 56

Comparison is Deadly 57

#7 We're Works in Progress 61

The Magic Word that Will Set You Free to Write 65

The Outer Game

7 Greenlights for Success - The Writer's Permission Slips............... 69

  #1 Permission to Do What Writers Do 73

    Engage with Your Imagination and Daydream 74

    Observe with Awareness 77

    Learn Craft.. 79

    Research 82

    Read... 84

    Doodle with Words for as Long as It Takes...................... 86

    The Secret Path to Calling Your Written Work DONE 87

  #2 Permission to Do It Your Way. 89

    The Value of Pauses 96

    Change the Scenery... 99

    Time is Arbitrary and On Your Side 102

  #3 Permission to Create and Have a Writing Space.................... 104

  #4 Permission to Choose What You Write 108

  #5 Permission to Own Your Superpower, Your Writer's Voice..... 112

  #6 Permission to Make Writing a Priority 117

  #7 Permission to Succeed by Your Definition of Success 119

The Truth About Stories 121

Your Best Creative Life - Living with Lasting Creative Freedom.. 125

  Lasting Creative Freedom - What is It? 126

  Envision Your Best Creative Life... 128

  Lasting Creative Freedom 130

  What Your Writing Means to You 132

  It's Never Too Late 140

  Your Ideal Writer's Life 142

  Your Perfect Day.. 147

  Other Writers, You Need Them 151

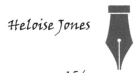

Rituals for Writing 154
Re-Imagine Your Creative Life 157
Claim Your Dreams 160

Conclusion 164

Your Creative Writer's Life Worksheet-Guide 167

Reader's Note 170

Acknowledgements 171

Idea Guide for a Writer's Life 174

THE WRITER'S BLOCK MYTH

Writer's block. The blank page. The thing labeled an affliction, a curse, a wall to break through. Search 'Writer's Block' on Amazon, and 100 pages show up. In the movie *Adaptation*, Nicolas Cage portrayed an anguished writer in the throes. I've been stuck, too. Overwhelmed. Lists circling my head. Writing time scheduled on the calendar that gets diverted to life, relationships, and other things, even laundry. I'm inspired with stories that need to go on paper in a life full of distractions. My goals and dreams looking so far away that I jump to thinking if only I had a finished book, I'd have permission to put some of the world on hold so I can immerse in what I love to write most. You know what I mean, right?

Then what happens is I start down the road of what's not there, looking at everything else in my life as stealing time away from writing, even when it's people or things I care about. And I freeze in anxiety or despair, hear the sad story of my life repeating itself in my head. I see myself as going nowhere. See myself as not good enough. Any rejection of my work, by myself or others, makes me wonder if I should give up.

Every person I've encountered—writers, artists, and those who don't write—has experienced being stuck, and knows what feeling blocked looks like. Everyone knows what it means.

Or do we?

From the time I was a small girl, artistic and creative expression was part of my life. My mother said I loved to draw and write from the moment I could hold a pencil. Paint, beads, mixed media, yarn, string, clay, paper, interior design, you name it. Fifteen years ago, when I committed to writing, I discovered a passion that not only surprised me, but married well my interest in psychology and sociology. What influenced me writing this book, though, were the conversations I had with other writers and the questions I heard at conferences and read in online forums. I realized that despite Google being our friend, most people didn't have the time or inclination, and perhaps not the patience or skill, to rout out solid information. Or to know how to vet what's useful or applies when creating a writing life. They need help beyond the sound advice for querying agents with the right letter. Because as more people took to their dream to write, the publishing world changed, and it continues to change fast.

Traditional publishing, once every author's aspiration, now rests under the umbrella of five large publishing and media corporations. Former independent publishers enfolded as imprints within the corporations. Many literary agencies consolidated to survive, or closed. A number of small presses moved to agent-represented submissions only. Tight budgets and lean staff in the industry narrowed the scope of work sought by both agents and publishers. An author platform, the body of readers and exposure in the marketplace an author develops, was elevated in importance across all genres of written works. At the same time, the number of Master of Fine Arts (MFA) full residency programs catering to writers grew from 148 to 229 in the four years between 2010 and 2014. Every student in those programs holding the dream of being a published author.

The upside is more writers in a tighter market has encouraged the growth of alternative publishing options. Self-publishing no longer carries the vanity press stigma as it once did. Online journals flourish, providing a forum for essays, short stories, and poetry to reach a broad audience. A spectrum of hybrid publishers that combine elements of support an author gets from a traditional house with the speed and agency of self-publishing has also emerged. Some offering marketing and author platform support, as well. Blogs have proliferated, and books developed from them. Readers sometimes contributing to the development of the stories. All providing a space for new genres, such as fan fiction, to emerge and a wide variety of writing styles to be showcased.

So, depending on what you read, publishing is harder with restricted options and more competition, or easier with more channels to do it yourself online and in print. Either way, navigating through a noisy world to write and be read with any degree of success can be challenging. Knowing why you write and what you want from your writing is more important than ever for nurturing a creative life.

But when the idea for this book first entered my mind, I pushed it aside. I was a novelist and poet, loving the journey of discovery in writing fiction, the rhythm and soul in poetry. I love the challenge of showing a reader what I see and hear in a story so they feel and see it, too.

As life goes, 2015 was a watershed year for me. I started a blog in March after years of resistance. In early fall I decided to amp up my work as a coach for writers, and one October evening, the title for this book shot through me so strongly I wrote it in the top margin of the page: **The Writer's Block Myth - Break Loose, Get Writing**. I sat with it, considered the title, how it reflects my core beliefs born from my own experience as an author and from my experience working with writers as an editor and coach. How our lives are inspiration for our writing, not resistance to it. I considered how we move forward quickly once perspectives or perceptions shift. That insights can come from inside us with the help of a guide. I knew this book had to be such a guide. That it had to include a chorus of other authors' voices. Because although writing is a solitary endeavor, authors need and want to hear from others who understand their experiences as writers.

I have a favorite blog about writer's block. It's by author Neil Gaiman in response to a reader who writes he has amazing ideas, but finds it hard getting thoughts onto paper and bringing his ideas to fruition. Neil Gaiman replies with logic—the only way to do is to do it. Then says *just kidding, there's much easier ways*. He goes on to narrate a convoluted, hilarious fairy tale about a magical tree on top of a distant mountain that produces five flowers one day a year, each blossom turning into a berry that ripens to a golden color, for which five white crows who have been waiting swoop down and pluck the berries. You must catch, with your bare hands, the smallest of the crows and wrangle the berry from it. He continues with the backstory about the crows and further instruction that for the next week you must speak to no one, nor sleep, but let the berry sit beneath your tongue. At midnight on the seventh day, you recite a tongue twister of a poem from the highest spot in your town, which is most likely a roof, while keeping the berry securely under your tongue. Then, and only then, you can swallow it and hurry home to fall into a deep sleep, and awake the next morning a writer. I imagine for some Neil Gaiman's tale may indeed sound like the easier path to being a writer. That balance and time and freedom to focus on writing can feel like a distant dream. The effort worth the rewards, but the journey sometimes challenging.

What I know is how you live your life is how your writing goes. That you aren't lazy when you're stuck and it's irrelevant there's no plumber's block or electrician's block, as some say for argument. Inspirational memes and exhortations that your stuckness is where the real creative work occurs won't help, at least not for long. Especially not when you're really stuck. And having another exercise you may or may not succeed in could backfire, add to your feelings of inadequacy or loss, perpetuating the downward spiral you may feel with your writing. In addition, willpower or putting your butt in the chair every day won't help when you feel pinched and caught between loved ones, your job, and obligations. There are writing bootcamps and National Novel Writing Month that will give you a kick to get going, but I don't see duress equating to an experience of lasting creative freedom either. Plus, I know thousands of words written without a book or essay or some framework that feeds a dream or goal can leave one feeling empty.

Then there's the question of your nature as a creative. How do you work best? What do you need to feel supported? What evidence gives you fresh perspectives? This is not to be confused with working only when inspired, but working in a way that considers who you are as a person so your strengths are empowered. The easiest example I have for this is the old adage, *you can't ask a fish to climb a tree.* Climbing a tree's not only outside a fish's abilities, but not in its nature.

My belief, and what I've seen in coaching writers, is that the best way to get unstuck is a change in perspective, at the same time recognizing that being stuck is more multi-faceted than fear, or bad habits, or failure to practice a prescribed way of doing things. We writers need approaches that don't shame, or leave us ungrounded, wondering how we nurture relationships *and* tend to our writing life. Different approaches to experiment with that include our everyday life in the process, not simply the page.

Writers want and need others to see them as writers. Need and want help dealing with the challenge of rejection that seeps inside, makes us shrink.

Because, let's admit it, when you've hit the wall, it doesn't help just to know every other writer occasionally hits the wall, too. You want to know how you stay on your feet and get through that wall. You want a way to remember those things you know deep down, like comparison is deadly, so you can turn your head straight, pull yourself back up. You want help when you're in the midst of the snarlies with your knees buckling under the layers of all the meaning you put on what you're doing and not doing. Strategies for moving forward and seeing progress. And when you're stumped, and you get up, fix yourself a cup of coffee or tea, throw another load of laundry in the machine, find yourself cleaning out the closet right afterward, you want to know in your heart you're still a writer.

Author Seth Godin says the "magic wand store" is closed. I agree. He suggests we ask the question, "What do you care enough about that you're prepared to expose yourself to fear, risk and hard work to get?" I think it's a good question, and for writers I offer that shifting perspectives and creating a writing life may be hard, but it doesn't have to *feel* hard. When you know what your writing means to you deep down in the center of our Being, it becomes a choice. And unless it's a slam into your body or up along the side of your head, change occurs in steps. And change is only truly noticed after a series of shifts occurs inside you. Getting past stuck and experiencing lasting creative freedom included.

Author Kim Barnes says writing is her life; she can't separate herself from it. She teaches at a university. Works with writers in workshops and at conferences. Always has a book or stories in the works. What I've heard from writers I interviewed is that many feel a split between their creative self and the one who takes care of the business of life and relationships with others. They struggle with balance. Even those who've made writing the center of their work in the world. Even Kim Barnes, who will go on retreat at times for space to write.

When I said *Yes, I'll write this book* to the Universe, I knew I wasn't alone in my moments of angst as a writer. But I wasn't sure if this was something others wanted now.

I conducted interview-conversations with writers as research. My sample was diverse. It included best-selling authors, school teachers, ghost writers, college professors, authors who've never published a thing, solo-preneurs, and business professionals. Both full-time and part-time writers. Some were authors I knew. Many were referrals after a conversation. All said *Yes* because they believe writers want and need this sort of support navigating the snarlies of life. Writers crave and need a boost from a grounded, holistic way to stay on our feet to create at our best.

Each conversation began with a request they share their relationship to writing. Followed by their biggest dream around writing, their frustrations, what they've done to support their writing life and address their frustrations, and how they feel writing fits in their lives now.

The reasons why they write vary—self-expression, personal inquiry, love of story, something inside them they can't ignore. Some feel writing saves them in the midst of hardships and difficulties, or offers a balance to their 'real' life by giving them a creative outlet and entry into another world. All felt writing was important and necessary to them, and all identified with being a writer. What I found interesting is those who started writing as an extension of their business and professional work are now writing personal stories they said they never would've considered before finishing a book as a product.

I learned our lives may look different on the outside, but as writers we consistently share the same frustrations. And the patterns may look different, but the labels we put on those frustrations vary little and line up into categories—Validation and Acceptance; Expectations that lead to focusing on a product and feeling lost to the process that satisfies them; Time and space to write; Distractions; Feeling split between writing and meeting the needs and obligations in everyday life; Needing permission to write. Everyone has felt stuck.

The interview-conversations verified all of us need something besides another failed promise of a magic bullet. We need a guide to find what works for us.

Tools that fit who *you* are as a writer and will work in *your* world. That can be carried with you as circumstances and relationships change. As you change.

We writers are a different breed. We are solitary creators. The fruits of our labor not readily visible to others upon completion. The complexity and skill of execution lost on those who have never tried to do it. Most people grow up reading, so they take for granted the brilliance of a good story. They don't know the 'training manual' is huge. That there are so many rules for how to do it *right*—engage a reader, spin the tale, paint the picture, get the idea across—and that we often must grow into it, mature as an author. And though our work is solitary, we need and value our nonsolitary lives populated by people and activities we may love equally because that life outside us not only provides love and meaning, but helps us be better writers.

"I don't think you can write according to a set of rules & laws;
every writer is so different."
~ Kiran Desai, author

These are some of the statements the writers I talked with shared. See what strikes a chord in you:

- ❖ I'd be validated and allowed time to write if I had a book or publication.
- ❖ They don't understand my need to write.
- ❖ My husband and friends don't understand why I would trade time with them for writing.
- ❖ It's constant decisions and negotiations between children, work, my husband, and writing. Every moment weighed.
- ❖ My skills as a writer are not valued or appreciated.
- ❖ I don't write as much as I should. I feel like a failure.
- ❖ I should be further along than I am.
- ❖ I keep asking myself, 'When can I finish this story?' I can't seem to get my manuscript done.
- ❖ I don't have enough skill.
- ❖ I don't have time to study or research for my book.
- ❖ I wonder if I'm self-sabotaging.
- ❖ How do I craft my life for me, and writing, and everything else, too?
- ❖ I feel I have no life and work balance. I'm never off the clock with work.
- ❖ I've lost my creative space.
- ❖ I can't find time for what I need.
- ❖ The groove I reach in summer breaks and vacations is truncated, interrupted, cut short.
- ❖ I feel guilty spending money for my writing. For conferences, classes, retreats, and other things I know will help.
- ❖ I have no psychic space to write.

- I have no time to dig deep into writing long enough to write a book.
- I can't seem to balance my writing with distractions and commitments.
- I'm afraid to let others read what I write.
- I have so many balls in the air; it's always stop and go.
- I work harder and longer rather than looking for my alignment to right action.
- I can't seem to let go of unfinished business.
- I sometimes think, 'Who do I think I am to be writing this story?'
- I have no one to talk to about writing or how I feel.
- I'm asked why I want to write a novel when I'm not a writer.
- Writing is a distraction from life, and life is a distraction from writing.
- I have two lives: my private life as a writer and my public life in my job.
- There's the person people think I am by what they see me do, and who I am.
- I never feel a sense of completion with my writing.
- There isn't a market for the kind of writing I want to do.
- I can't be a writer. There are too many stressors in my life. I'm overwhelmed.
- I have ideas. I don't know how to begin.
- I question my path as a writer. I wonder if I should be doing something else.
- Remembering the joy I find in writing gets me unstuck and moving, but it can be hard remembering it.
- I don't have a space for just me and my writing.
- I work best in isolation, without distractions, and that space is hard to find.
- I'm a perfectionist.

❖   I question how I can craft my life so writing fits.

❖   When I'm stuck and spinning my wheels, I question myself.

❖   Not writing costs me my peace.

---

*"The important question is how much peace and time being
YOU do you want in your life.
~ Sweetie Berry, author*

Change happens in a series of shifts. The quantum leap often coming somewhere down the road from when the first shift occurs. What works for other writers may not work for you. This is a guide to help you experience lasting creative freedom, your way.

Let me tell you a story. 5:00 a.m., I'm sitting in a tiny airport in Saint John's, New Brunswick, Canada, waiting for my 5:30 a.m. flight. I am returning home after ten days touring and interviewing innkeepers for a possible venue where I might host a writers' retreat. Next to me, a gal on her phone. Not a wisp of tired in her voice for so early in the morning. I hear *design, jeans, overseas.* Clearly a business call.

In line to board the plane, we strike a conversation. I learn she has a degree in art, is now partner in a clothing company, and is a frequent flier. "Gotta make a living," she says. When I tell her about my book, she immediately says every artist needs this book. And that she'd only known one artist who never felt blocked. "All through school, every single person had times feeling stuck, but he never did," she said. "He never stressed over his work." I leaned in.

"What he did," she said, "was paint the same thing over and over every day until something moved." A light flashed inside me. I'd done the same thing while writing my second novel! For months I wrote the same spot in the story. The same conflict. Like a dance around a small floor, going in circles despite different prompts, another day, or insights upon waking. I didn't hesitate or falter in the writing. I was in flow like he was, but I saw it differently than he did. I saw myself stuck. I didn't accept what I did as good enough. I thought myself flawed, blocked. Having lost the heart of the work, the juice. What I realized from her story is he knew what I didn't. The creative's inner game was in his bones. He knows his work is supported and stimulated by feeling open and expansive inside, as well as by what he does. And he knew this was the genius of moving forward. That it was his key to lasting creative freedom. Whereas I didn't understand those fine points, at all. I thought about this for days.

My remembered experiences of writer's block go back to third grade. I can still see the open-air lunch room at a school in southern California. I can still place myself on the bench at the dark brown table where I composed four lines on white paper with a pencil. I remember I sought rhyme, because poems rhymed. Remember my prompt was a student's poem in a newsletter and that I had an aspiration for the same, deciding a poem something I could do. I like to believe it was more primal. The birth of the lyrical style in my adult works, perhaps. I did love to sing often. I remember feeling unsure of its worth. Questioning if I truly created a poem. I didn't show the poem to my teacher or submit it to the school newsletter.

That same year I planned a volume of short stories at home. I completed a table of contents and five of the tales before abandoning it like I did the poem.

At eleven I won recognition for a long story I wrote. The pages were displayed on a table at a school arts fair. At twelve, my teacher wrote *good in creative writing* on my report card, and I attended a Student Authors' Tea.

But at eighteen I hit the wall that shut me down for decades. I flunked creative writing in college. Every Friday we sat for the hour, our only assignment to write. And each week I dropped a blank sheet of paper on the professor's desk. In later years, writers I shared this with lauded me my bravery and defiance. The truth was I didn't know what to write or how to begin. I was paralyzed with no tools for getting through it.

After that, I put my creative energy entirely into visual art-making. Confined my words to postcards and inconsistent journal entries, until age twenty-seven when I suffered a painful divorce.

Like angels and birds, poems flew to me unbidden as I transitioned through fear in the dissolution of my marriage and faced challenges as a single parent of a young child. Perfectly rhymed chronicles of my heart and thoughts spontaneously sprung from my pen whenever I journaled. Often in the middle of the night as I lay awake. For three years they came. Then as suddenly as they arrived, they left. My stronger heart no longer needing succor, I suppose.

In the ensuing years I wrote academic papers, promotional copy, proposals, and training manuals for classes and jobs. I was an activist focused on the establishment of a Women's Center on a major university campus, credited with a gift for speaking and writing. But six years after I graduated, I realized I'd lost my voice and writing abilities as if some part of me melted away. I joined a circle of women, wrote from prompts and shared. Oh, it was hard. Not the writing, but leaving the group mute when we went around the circle reading our raw work. I received no nods, grunts of approval, or comments like the other writers got. I wanted to quit, but was encouraged to stay with it. I practiced, studied, and learned to get out of my own way. In that period, I learned to accept my writer's Voice and call myself a writer. And I wrote a novel.

In 2009, my husband was run down by a car as a pedestrian. I became his caretaker, patient advocate, and expert on insurance and legalities. In all the fray, I did not lose my identity as a writer. I still said aloud to myself and others—I am a writer. But I turned to the other things writer's do, which I talk about later in the book.

In 2011, my life circumstances changed drastically, again. The medicine of poetry flew in like birds and angels once more. This time, the poetry of nature out my windows. I watched the cycles of life on the St. Johns River cross the seasons. Tracked weather, reflections, and light across the forever sky and changing tides. Gazed into sky canyons like alternate universes on the water's surface. I composed short, poetic descriptions of all I observed on Facebook as a writing practice, editing them with care. I wanted each post to say *join me, see and feel this with me*. And one day, standing at water's edge on Tampa Bay as the sun rose, the line of a poem rang in my head - I stand at the altar of birds. I wove my poetic Facebook posts with new stanzas, shaped them into a poem that was nominated for a Pushcart Prize in 2014.

Today I know it never was writer's block in those times between the big moments of triumph and the big moments when my writing ground to a halt, leaving me feeling stuck. Writer's block is a symptom of Life Block, and as writers, it shows up most in our relationship with the page. At the point where we *see* the manifestation of something blocking our way to a goal or our Soul's calling. And often, writing's far less threatening than the challenges we face in life. So, we lose or let go of our writing because we can. It may leave you feeling awful, but for most writers, even those who call themselves professional, writing does not pay the bills. And it doesn't hold up in others' eyes as a substitute for time with family or friends, or careers and household. Unfortunately, the awful feeling in your gut is your creative soul in pain. I understand.

The Inner Game

7 Keys to Set You Free to Write

One warm winter Florida morning, I noticed a strange little rainbow off the window sill in my kitchen where it shouldn't be. A little six-inch rod of color. I looked around for the source, but nothing made sense. While in that pause before the full start of my day, I watched the colors fade, and the heart of what being an author taught me about life swept through my mind like a gorgeous cosmic download. Stunned, I grabbed a pen, jotted it all down in a list as fast as I could. The details fading along with the rainbow.

As time passed, I saw that morning's inspiration was the foundation to a successful writer's inner life. That every one of the things I jotted down was a point at which a writer might fall off the cliff into self-doubt, questioning herself and feeling challenged. Even feeling caught in a choice between life in the 'real' world and her creative life. The kind of challenges to one's sense of self as a writer that could cause a halt to writing or pursuing aspirations. One might even put down their pen, quit writing forever without ever realizing the keys to this inner game can be filed on a shelf in the heart or mind. That we can learn to recognize them, get what we need to keep going, even when each point may be a boulder to trip on, leaving us feeling stuck in life, experiencing writer's block.

There are two old truths we often forget. One, it's not how often we falter or fall, but how fast we get up. And two, the creative life *is* our 'real' life.

Let me tell you how I know this. I've always loved the language of life in stories and pictures, but I never thought I'd be an author. My work in the world was diverse, including positions as a corporate advertising account manager, micro-brewery owner building a business, activist creating a women's center on a large university campus, clay artist, and manager of school and family programs in an art museum. When I joined a women's writing circle in 2002, writing to prompts and sharing our raw work (the same group I wanted to quit over and over), I found a refuge from the snarlies of life. No matter what was going on in my life, those two and a half hours were mine. And believe me, my evidence journal was proof I needed to step outside my everyday life. Over the next several years, I experienced a home remodel going $120,000 over budget with an absentee contractor, being stalked, holding together a business, a husband run down by a car, a house on fire, and job losses. So, when I closed the door to my life, sat present to my writing with the other women, I was on retreat. And when I was invited to a weeklong writers' retreat, terrified I wouldn't write a thing during our free afternoons, I wrote a short story every afternoon the entire week not realizing this didn't happen for most writers. And when I grew curious, I followed the first story I wrote at the weeklong retreat about a little boy growing up alone in mid-century rural Appalachia, a prophecy, and a mother coming to terms with her heartache and choices. I had no expectations when I followed that story. I thought perhaps I was writing a novella when I reached 20,000 words. At 50,000 words, I knew I was writing a novel and saw myself fully as a writer. I liked it. The process was exciting. When I was done with the book, I did what I was supposed to do as an author. I found beta readers for my novel from generations in the region who could tell me if I got it right from my research and heart. Because, although I had lived in the mountains for years, felt a kinship with the area and people from there, I grew up in big cities far from Appalachia and I wanted the work true. I next hired a professional editor, got advance praise quotes from bestselling authors, created an author website to the wisdom of the day, centered around the book. I submitted short works to journals and anthologies for publication so I had something to put on my query letter. Three weeks after beginning my search for a literary agent, I had one. He had years in the business, represented New York Times bestselling authors, and was so enthusiastic about my book that he submitted to the best editors in New York first. I started my second novel. Continued taking classes, going to conferences and retreats. By the time my agent and I amicably split, I had a folder full of praise from New York editors for my writing, my characterization, and my knowledge of the craft, but no publishing deal. I'd done everything right and it didn't matter. We didn't know the environment in the publishing industry was changing for everyone.

In the midst of this journey with my book, my home caught on fire, displacing me for five months, and my husband was run down by a car while he walked on a sidewalk one gorgeous fall morning. I stopped writing. But I loved my characters, believed in my book. I loved writing and all things authorly. I didn't understand so much of what I was doing—reading, studying, research, observing with awareness—also equaled writing (something we'll talk about in the next section). I simply held on to my Writer Self despite not looking much like a writer to anyone on the outside looking in.

I turned to understanding the publishing industry, became a scholar. Eventually turned to teaching and consulting others in how they might best move forward to meet their writing goals. In time I began writing full-time again. On occasion diving into my novel in progress, but mostly writing poetry and essays. My intent that one day I'd return to my first love, longform fiction. The form where I dream the most in the process and feel most engaged with the joy of discovery.

So, when years later I got that cosmic download, I recognized it for what it was. The keys to life that translate to the keys to getting past stuck as a writer. I understood writer's block is a myth, because it's a symptom of what's going on in your life. Even when it's the story or ideas you believe you're fighting.

You've heard these seven keys before. Probably know each one intimately in your head. But it takes a shift inside you to move to an automatic alignment of relationship to the page when you're stuck. The thing to remember is it doesn't have to be hard. Not when you're clear what you want. Sometimes it's as simple as changing a word in the way you talk to yourself.

Writing is always a tad bigger than we are. Writing the story with all the elements that make it whole and complete a tad bigger still. In the midst of writing, you can feel good and not so good at the same time. Just as whenever you're living intentionally, engaging in a dance with creativity in the process and the stretch sometimes feels almost too hard to do. These are the times you shift into aspiring to meet your best story, whether inside you or on the page. So you experience not a weight, but a light inside you that you reach for. This is the writer's inner game.

Look for short, easy guides and things to do for awareness, reflection, and to get past stuck at the end of most sections. Short, because time is precious, right? Simple, because the brain likes simple, and the brain wants a *Win*, whether we know or not ahead of time there's no losing. So, if you've done some of these short, easy things before, do them again. This is a journey. You're not in the same place you were a day ago, a week ago, or a month ago, no matter what you think or feel. . .because you are alive! Everything you do here is a step in shifting toward living and loving your best creative life, and experiencing lasting creative freedom.

---

*"I came to realize that the new narrative was just
the flip side of the old narrative."*
~ *Nancy Peacock, author*

KEY #1

Pay attention to the Evidence Journal.

We all have an evidence journal. It's where we notate our accomplishments, gifts, strengths, weaknesses, and hot buttons. Where we tally and backlog all the reasons why what we believe and profess are true. Our evidence journal stores the validity of both our triumphs and our pain. Shows us the disconnects between our intents and what gets done. It tells us who's paying attention and sees us, as well as who's dismissed us. Everything we need to know is in the evidence journal. Yet, for something so important it's rarely a physical book or sheaf of papers, but most often kept in our head. The hard part as humans, and even harder for creatives, is seeing and keeping up with everything there. It's as if we're selectively blind. We often see what supports our fears and insecurities. We'll writhe in the affirmation, call it Truth. Because it's where we hurt. Like a scraped right knee, we forget the left knee that is perfectly fine. We sink into the pain, give it our attention. Worst of all, we discredit the small things we do as not enough rather than acknowledge how the pieces fit in the bigger picture of our lives.

Does this sound overly dramatic? Think about it in relation to your writing life. When you feel like you're two people, the writer and the one others may say you are that challenges you writing, what do you do? Do you close the door and write anyway? If you do, good for you! Do you feel guilt or dismissed, and let those feelings hamper you writing? If yes, look closely at what your evidence journal says. Did you write at all? Have you written even one page in the past month? Did you think about your project? Writing involves more than pen to paper or fingers on the keyboard. It involves noticing, observing with awareness, research, dreaming, one hundred pages written for those twenty pages of gems. It involves breathing between the words. Writer's write, knowing that others may not understand. And writers do all the other things that go into making a writer.

Here's a warning about evidence journals. . . since they're most often kept in your head, they're incomplete. Every instance is not noted. Pieces are missing. So it's easy to fall into the trap of seeing what's not there and what hurts, rather than everything actually present and true.

Start with awareness. When you feel you have no time to write, look at your evidence journal for when you have time, whether it's ten minutes or an hour. When you feel overwhelmed, buried under everything that needs doing, look at the evidence journal for what you've done already as an affirmation you're not standing still. Avoid judgment, and search out the space in your life—predictable space, space between daily tasks, space in others' schedules where you're not urgently needed. Include space you give yourself—quiet time alone in the morning or late at night, massages, vacations, retreats, reading a book. If you don't give yourself space, ask why not and start! This is your life.

Something easy

Keep a physical evidence journal. It can be a sheet of paper, a small book you carry around, a notebook that stays open on the kitchen counter. Make it something easy that works for you.

Write down the pages or sentences you wrote and the minutes you spent thinking or writing on your project. Write down what you particularly noticed that day, such as the color of a child's tee-shirt, or the way the sunlight fell across the table, or an overheard conversation, or the items in a shopping cart in front of you at the grocery store. Write down research you've done, including quotes you saw on Facebook, articles or a novel you read that informs your craft or your project. What you put in your personal journal counts as writing, too.

Note the spaces in your life, without judgment. Be curious about how long and what sort of space you have. It doesn't matter if it's three minutes or an hour. Was it waiting time, predicable time, time that shows up unexpectedly? Look for patterns, such as the time of day, day of the week, who's with you and who isn't. Is it always the same? Does it vary? How? Why? Note how you fill that space. Is it running to cram one more thing in from your list? Is it daydreaming? Is it worrying or fretting that hogs all the space in your brain and air in your lungs? You don't have to spend a lot of time doing this. Just note and notice. No right, wrong, good, bad.

Now, take a few moments after a day or two or three. Look at what's happening versus what's not happening, what's there versus what's not there. Where does space show up in your life? Where could there be space? How is it different than what you thought it looked like? Or if it looks the same as you thought it would, notice what else may be there. Notice what things you can forgive or change.

Feel how much easier it is to look at your daily life this way. Find where you feel it in your body. Deep down feel it. Turn your focus to that place in your body and notice long enough so you recognize the feeling.

If it still feels hard to see space or time in your life, ask for help from someone who will support you as a writer. Ask them what they see.

I underline the importance of asking someone who doesn't challenge you as a writer or your feelings in any way. This eliminates anyone who may not understand your need to write, regardless of how close that person may be to you. Save that particular conversation about understanding your need to write for later. Right now, you want support.

Your mind is not a lost calf. You can gently wrangle it. You can shift your sights to possibilities.

KEY #2

Let go of dead-end distractions, and do what answers Yes.

In our written work, dead-end distractions are the sidebars and 'smoking gun' exposition in a scene that takes us out of the action. They're the backstory that slogs down the narrative, or leaves a reader asking *so what?* It's the subplots that don't tie-in, or rambling in the telling that renders a reader bored. In life, they're the things that take us away from what we believe we want, and often the things we ignore that help us feel whole. They may be shoulds and oughts given us over time that become our stories, or shoulds and oughts that enter our lives with our relationships, job, or circumstances. They can include things that are important to us—family, obligations, responsibilities, a tug of enjoyment, friends. It's easy to forget dead-end distractions have nothing to do with the value of what you let go of. That we're talking about what takes you *away* from what makes you feel whole, and it's not all or nothing. For writers, this includes taking us away from the things writers do besides putting pen to paper, too.

Remember the artist who did the same thing every day and never felt blocked? He let go of the dead-end distraction of expecting what he should produce. Think what this means for you. Is a neat home important? Find a way to have it without costing you time on your goal. Ask for help or hire someone, even once a month for two hours. Is time with friends important? Schedule it around your sacred time with yourself and your writing. If work demands overwhelm you, step away, take a walk, or take a day off for no reason if you can afford it and engage with your writing life. Have lunch alone where you can write. One thing that works for me when distractions feel impossible is a minute with my eyes closed, my focus on my breath. Not on my writing or anything outside myself. I focus on the simplicity of my breath as a way to enter a state of calmness. Sometimes I'll lie on the sofa for ten minutes, call it a sanctioned pause without guilt or stress. Sometimes I'll simply say aloud, "What do I need now?" and follow my inclination. Only after I'm calm do I direct my inner vision to what I'm writing.

What you're doing in this process is looking for the threads you can unravel and weave back differently in your life. You're centering into yourself as a writer in the midst of all that swirls around you that you call your life, and creating Peace (with a capital P) inside you.

Do what answers Yes.

Do what answers Yes. Yes expands inside you. Yes opens you to your creative spirit while a heavy-on-the-heart No restricts your creative spirit.

Give yourself permission to say No to those who drain you or demand your time when you need to write. Sometimes this is difficult. It could be your children, spouse, partner, or friend. What you want to remember is it's only a brief time that you've declared for yourself. You're finding a balance that works for you and seeking expansion for something that's important to you. This is not selfish. It's the oxygen mask you put on yourself first.

This sort of No is an 'aligned No.' Meaning it rings inside you like a Yes as an affirmation for what you really want if there was no weight of rejection or obligation or fear. Aligned No's are a powerful practice for all aspects of your life.

Add more Yes and aligned No's to your life.

 ## *Something easy*

Start noticing how it feels when you do something where your first thought is No. Notice where you feel it in your body, and what happens with your thinking and emotions.

Notice how it feels when you do something where your first thought is Yes. Notice how much calmer your thoughts are. How much more expansive and creative you feel with the Yes.

Practice saying aligned No's. Notice how empowered you feel once you get over the discomfort of doing something so new to you. Once the fear and guilt you adopted dissipates.

Schedule 10-minute mini-retreats where anything goes as long as it's about you and your writing. Which means, as long as you're doing what writers do: daydream and imagine, observe with awareness, learn your craft, research, accept your process with the knowledge it takes as long as it takes (we'll talk more about what writers do in Part Two).

Schedule your mini-retreats once a day, twice a week, or on whatever schedule you *know* you can meet. Use a kitchen timer so you're not

---

distracted looking at the clock or your watch. If sound is a difficult distraction, listen to white noise through earphones. There are a number of apps you can download to your phone. Do not listen to music unless your writing practice includes music.

* Write in your evidence journal. Pay attention.

KEY #3

Trust the permeable boundaries of the creative process.

All writers are creative. Storytellers and poets creating word pictures and touching the senses. Journalists and business leaders imparting facts and reportage. Essayists supporting opinions and subjective response to something outside or inside themselves. Unskilled writers, as well as skilled writers. Because the act of putting words together in sentences, sentences together into paragraphs, paragraphs into a whole that engages a reader requires thinking, intuition, and consideration beyond the dynamics of an A to B destination with set guidelines. It requires thought that connects to the many aspects of being human.

Though it may seem contradictory when you consider thought, skillsets, and craft, creativity is not about control. We want control of our instruments and tools, but true creativity involves openness to the unknown and letting go of what we've decided to look for or expect to find in the work. It happens when we soften our focus and allow ourselves to be stretched beyond our present knowledge and perceptions so we're carried into the realm where ah-ha's occur. Such as when the story takes an unintended direction, or an unplanned image appears in the middle of a verse, or a new detail shows up in our research. It happens when we cross the permeable boundaries of creativity that neither hardline thinking nor strict determination allows. Oh, gosh, I know all this, you may say. But ask yourself, "Where is my focus when I write?"

When you let yourself be truly open without expectation and judgment, you realize your creativity never asks your permission to be there or express itself. It only asks you accept whatever shows up for consideration. I add, feel lucky when you follow it, for that's where you may have the most fun. Whew, hard. Right?

Think about this. . .you have a story you're going to tell. You know the way you're going to tell it. You may even know the rules you aren't supposed to break. May even have a message. But what if something wonderful is there you hadn't thought about? What if you didn't know you had a new way of telling that story, or that there were more layers to that story than you envisioned or thought? What if you didn't think about it, and followed the story or the rhythm of random words until you settled into the process and saw where it led?

"I've had a sign over my typewriter for over 25 years now,
which reads Don't Think!"
~ Ray Bradbury

Get Curious

Sometimes the best way past stuck is to simply get curious. This approach is particularly effective if you've completed a project and ready to write again, but unsure what's next. Let your curiosity carry you into new, interesting territory with your writing, leading to engagement, wonder, questioning, or exploration.

Elizabeth Gilbert tells the story in her book *Big Magic* about a time she wanted to write and found nothing coming to mind. She asked herself again and again if there was *anything* she was interested in, even a tiny bit, and was completely surprised when gardening came up. Though she'd been in the vegetable garden with her mother while growing up, it was something that touched nothing inside her inherent self or past interests. It was more a whim. But she followed it with curiosity and planted some flowers. Memories surfaced as she worked the soil, carried her to thinking about the women in her family before her. As the garden grew, she saw it with different eyes and discovered she wanted to *know* about the plants, not just cultivate them. Specifically, she wanted to know where the plants came from. This led to an online search about one of the flowers in her garden, an heirloom iris, whose origin was Syria. A fact so surprising to her that she looked into the origins and history of other plants, which led to a newfound interest of botanical history. Her newfound interest led to travel, new people, and investigation that became a passion she had no idea she would have. Ultimately her new passion became the research for her next novel, *The Signature of All Things*. The female protagonist in the book linking back to Gilbert's early thoughts about the heritage of women before her. Her entire journey to the novel evolving from a Yes to a tiny, unexpected curiosity.

One author I spoke with says she's always looking for a new challenge, and while doing research for a book to write, a story came to her that she feels passionate about and can't ignore. It not only incorporates both her background as an MD and her interests in women's accomplishments, but requires extensive research, work natural and easy to her as it's a huge part of her profession. With the confluence of all these elements, the story feels as if it holds aspects of her in it. She followed her curiosity to the novel no one but she can write.

Curiosity was what led to me writing my first novel, too. I was curious what happened next in that first story I wrote at my first writing retreat. I was curious about whether I could follow the boy, because I didn't know if I had the skill to write a longer work. That was the first story I'd written since I was a schoolgirl! All I had to work with was a ten-year-old boy named Jamie, his abusive stepfather Redmond, his distant mother Sarah, a stranger in the hollow named Jack, and a meeting that held promise. That was it. But I was curious about these characters. I wanted to know them. Wanted to know their stories. What I learned is I'm an intuitive writer who follows the work rather than leads. I listen to the characters and see scenes in my mind's eye. The entire process writing the novel turned into an experience of following curiosity. Many scenes written from prompts without thought or intention, taking me in surprising directions. Many times leaving me confused because what I wrote seemed to contradict the story or what I knew of the place and time. When it first happened, I'd resort to research as confirmation I heard the story right before proceeding. Later I trusted the process, and kept writing until the pieces fell into place so it made sense. It could seem crazy, but it was fun. I was totally immersed in the adventure.

To illustrate how literally I mean this. . .toward the end of the book I started a chapter sure the boy Jamie would find his mother in the room. But when I wrote the beginning of the scene, she wasn't there. I was so surprised I stopped writing, not sure what to do before I realized I had to keep going to find out where she was. At another point in the book, I cried as I wrote. My husband saw me, asked what was wrong. "The ending. It's so beautiful," I said. "But you're writing the book. You know the ending," he said. "No," I told him. "I didn't know *this*." I followed my curiosity and let myself be led to something I never could've written otherwise.

Any time you're stuck, drop back, relax. Be led by curiosity in a way that works for you.

To be creative, don't look for something.
Look For Anything.
~ Anthony, 13-years-old (from his tiny book, How to be Creative)

Let Go of Expectations

Let go of expectations. Stop the futile seeking of certainty that can't be found, as Seth Godin says. Step into the realm of allowing yourself to be surprised and led to something new. Step into the *process* of writing. Don't wait for a feeling of applause inside yourself. You have your intent. Your story is there. You know what you're doing. Even the structure you thought you'd follow is still there. Your creativity listens to intent, and dances with it. Expands the dance floor.

Think how bad it feels when you don't meet your expectations. You can feel let down, not good enough, even beat yourself up. Today, let go of expectations. Tell yourself you're simply going to follow the pen.

Wait! I want to dance with my creativity, but I'm stuck. I don't feel creative.

Where's your focus? Is it on the book, or the scene you have to write? Is it on that story, or article you want to submit? Is it on a product, or on process? Focused on the end result, or on the present?

Creativity is about the process of writing and allowing whatever shows up in. Remember, your intent defines the dance with creativity you're doing. If you're only focusing on the product or final result of the work while you're engaged in creating, you can get stuck because you're not in the zone of creativity and creating.

A side note. . .sometimes we get stuck because we're trying to stay with a story or work that just isn't ours to tell. This, again, is focusing on the expectation: *I will tell this story; if I just stick with it, I will find a way in.* If after the second draft you're still not feeling it—character, direction, joy in the process—step back, ask yourself if this story or work is yours to write.

Let me give you an example how I regularly dance with creativity. Every Tuesday morning, I post a blog called *Getting to Wise. A Writer's Life.* The posts are much like this book in that they're stories about shifting my perspectives to get past stuck and pick myself up to move forward again. My insights often come while writing the blog. At this point, my only intention each week is being present and open to how life creatively plays out. But when I started the blog, I didn't have a clue about any of this. My first thought when I looked at that first blank screen was *a quote is always good.* I wrote one of my favorites, "When you're in motion, the form will appear," by Michael Hyatt. *That's appropriate*, I thought. Then I chose a picture from dozens taken on my dawn walks to Tampa Bay. And I thought of something that had happened recently which made me aware how solidly those dawn walks sustained me. I wrote it in a way that was fun for me. Meeting the challenge of capturing the magic and feelings I experienced each morning. It was short, sweet, complete, and garnered a dozen emails from friends and acquaintances as well as thirty-two shares on Facebook. . .when I had no subscribers, yet. My blog struck a chord inside people, which felt like a huge triumph. The point is I had an intention, and I let creativity take the reins. That was on March 18, 2015.

Within weeks someone told me I wrote small journeys. Another reader said I shared how to navigate through life. I let that be my unconscious intention, and the question I'd check was answered at the end. Over time I accepted I didn't know what the blog would specifically be about until I started. I only know that whatever was up inside me the previous week will be the focus, and by the end of the blog I'd have taken a journey, ended with an ah-ha moment. I sometimes wonder if the nature of the blog will change. I trust if it does, I'll be guided by the creative process in that, too.

So, let go of worrying about submitting and publishing while you're writing. Let go of striving to be better as the words flow. There's a time for that. Let go of what you think you're going to write. Right now, breathe into your creative process.

"When I sit down with an act of will, either before the typewriter or to pray, I have to let go of my control and listen. I listen to the story or I try to get beyond the words of prayer and listen to God. Ultimately when I hear, that is the gift, not my act of will, not my act of virtue. It is pure gift."
– Madeleine L'Engle

 ### *Something easy*

Make a list. What's on it doesn't matter. It can be a list of vegetables, the colors you see around you, flowers you can think of, all the meals you ate the past week, animals in the zoo, or the little things people do. It doesn't matter, but it's best to go with the first thing that pops in your mind. And don't get stuck on keeping to how you first defined the list. Your list of flowers can have 'elephant' in it.

Chose one item from the list as a prompt. Write for 5 to 15 minutes without pauses to think, ponder, or correct. Let mistakes happen and leave them as you wrote them. No worries about spelling or grammar or anyone seeing what you write. If a story emerges, be surprised without trying to have it make sense. This is about letting go of expectations and control, and allowing creativity to take the reins. Your only intention is to be present.

Schedule time for this each day. If that feels like too much to promise yourself, or a sure thing to fail, do it every other day or twice a week. Just 5 to 15 minutes. Put it on your calendar, or do whatever you do that helps you keep your appointments with yourself. Three rules:

1. Write without stopping.
2. No editing, judging, or trying to figure out what you're writing.
3. Write with pen and paper. No keyboard. Editing is not part of the process, and keyboards make us natural editors. Trust it enough to love it while you're there. Feel it the same way a hug can be with someone you love. You may not be in their arms all the time, but it stays with you.

If you get stuck in this process, simply write "what am I trying to say" or "blah blah blah" and keep going. You *will* dive down into it, again. And so you know you're in good company, Maya Angelou said she liked to write her way out of stuck, forcing herself to put words—any words—on paper until she reached the other side.

There will be times when you don't dive back in right away, too. Those blah blah blah's will lie like an ugly string on the page. That's okay, too. You're following, not leading. Practice allowing creativity to join your intention.

"You can only write regularly if you're willing to write badly. You can't write regularly and well. One should accept bad writing as a way of priming the pump, a warm-up exercise that allows you to write well."
~ Jennifer Egen, Pulitzer prize-winning author

Add each minute you write to your evidence journal.

* Pay attention to the evidence journal
* Notice your Yes's
* Schedule and take 10 minute retreats

There are no rules for the best way to approach your writing, no matter what butt-in-the-chair people say. It's important to find the rhythm that works for you. And leaves you feeling good, as if you've won something, even when it's imperfect. You want wins!

So, if writing every day is hard to meet successfully, schedule a sacred hour or two a week. One to two hours where you turn off your phone and distractions, devote yourself to writing. Everything else scheduled before or after. Remember, we once lived in a world where people couldn't reach us every second of our lives. If you have kids, enlist them to help. Have the oldest be a monitor at your door or give them a creative task of their own to share when all of you are done.

You can do this. How often or how long you write is not the important thing. Only that you write. If you still have questions, consider I completed a third of my novel by writing once a week in a circle of women from prompts while my life seemed to crash down around me.

The only thing that makes life possible is
permanent, intolerable uncertainty:
not knowing what comes next.
Ursula K. Le Guin (The Left Hand of Darkness)

KEY #4

Connection is alchemical.
Writing is connection.

For us writers, connection is that space between the written words and ourselves, and between the written words and the reader. The connection in the spaces is where our most intimate conversation as writers occurs. It's where relationship and impact grow because it starts with 'me' and ends with 'us,' creating something bigger than we were a moment before.

At the same time, though it may sound contradictory, what you do can be great and expansive even if no one sees it. Thousands of fine sentences no one will read. Hundreds of kindnesses no one will know about. Because writing is the thing you do that calls to your heart and brings you to life, as author Elizabeth Gilbert says. Another's eyes don't make it more or less than it is.

Poet and Pulitzer Prize nominee Jack Gilbert knew this. He had all the makings of a literary star—charisma, passion, brilliance, and irresistible appeal to both men and women. He wrote beautiful poetry that made people want more, but he was indifferent to fame. He rejected it as full of distractions and stepped away from the limelight. For two decades he lived in Europe, wrote in private. When he resurfaced and published another collection of poetry, the world fell in love with him all over again. And once more he disappeared. This time for ten years. He repeated the pattern his entire life. His students from a temporary teaching position he once held at the University of Tennessee, Knoxville remembered him as living in a "state of uninterrupted marvel." Uninterrupted marvel, writing words no one would see until he held them out like gifts to the world, asking nothing in return.

Every person desires touch in one form or another. A meeting with something or something other than themselves. Jack Gilbert found it, but not in fame. Poet and author David Whyte describes touch in his book, *Consolations: The Solace, Nourishment and Underlying Meaning of Everyday Words*, as a core experience of presence and the willingness to be touchable. He says if we are not in relationship, we have retreated from the world and drawn the boundaries of our imaginations and minds into a small circle about us. Some, even many, find touch by this definition through solitude and nature. Many in relationships. Writers always through writing.

I posit that the connection in the space between the words and the reader is your gift to the world, and to yourself. Author and entrepreneur Seth Godin carries it a bit further when he talks about creating something and offering it to another. He says the four words 'Here, I Made This' carry generosity (here), intent (I made), risk, and intimacy (this) in them. And the more we say these four words and mean them, and deliver on them, the more art and connection we create. A cycle of giving to others that also gives to us.

You are sparking life inside yourself when you write. You are sparking life in others when they read and connect with your work. This connection through writing is a wellspring for your life.

As between the words, there is space in your life.

Something easy

Turn your gaze to the smallest moments and actions that leave you feeling satisfied with yourself. View each as a step toward your goals. See every one as a triumph, not a failing or something less than intended, whatever the result from the action. And give yourself a high five. Notice how space opened around your heart and inside your mind with that high five.

Each time a little space opens in your life or you feel satisfaction in a triumph, write it down on a piece of paper. Put that piece of paper in a jar or bowl. Place the jar or bowl where you can see it.

Every time you feel your insides tighten, look at those pieces of paper in the jar as your evidence, your reminders you have space in your life and inside you.

- Pay attention to the evidence journal
- Notice your Yes's
- Schedule and take 10 minute retreats
- Write 5 to 10 minutes from a prompt

KEY #5

Rejection happens,
so cheer the triumphs.
Triumphs are everywhere every day.

I want to sing like birds sing, not worrying who
hears or what they think.
~ Rumi

The level of rejection authors experience would astonish most people. Sometimes (often) hundreds of rejections, often year after year.

We hear about the big winners. Rarely do we read they are less than 1 percent of published authors or that the average sales for self-published books are 150 - 250 copies. Or that good writers are not immune to rejection. Nor bestselling authors.

Rejection frequently has nothing to do with the work. Publishing is a subjective business. A look behind the scenes at a publishing deal with one of the big five traditional publishing houses (called the Big Five) reveals a deal requires buy-in from the marketing department, as well as approval from the managing editor. Considerations such as how the book fits in the upcoming house catalog, how it can be marketed, what in-house author will the new author compete with, and the author's platform play in the decision. In addition, a thorough profit-loss analysis is projected for the work. Small publishers and literary journals may publish a book the Big Five turns away, but their budgets are limited and they're very selective since the number they publish each year is so few. Often less than a dozen volumes a year. Every professional in the industry looks at your creation as a product to market and sell. The creation containing your heart and soul that has squeezed sweat from your brow and consumed hours, perhaps years. The agent sells it to a publishing acquisitions editor. The acquisitions editor sells it to the marketing department and managing editor. And these two people have to love it enough to meet whatever challenge arises in the process.

Rejection can also come from critiques by other writers, and may sting. Remember to take what works, consider the rest, leave what doesn't work after you do. You're the author. A helpful tact with critique is after you've absorbed the feedback, put it aside for a week or a month. Revisit it later with new eyes when you're past any sting. And remember, good critique that objectively applies to your work is a learned skill, and not all writers have that skill. So, be discerning in your response to the feedback you receive.

This probably is closest to hitting 'home' for many writers. I'll share two experiences I had to illustrate how valuable this tact of non-attachment and letting critique rest can be. One where I was the recipient. Another where I gave the critique.

As I was writing my novel *Flight*, author Valerie Ann Leff was in my writing circle and heard the raw drafts of many scenes. When I completed the book, she offered to read it and share with author Ron Rash for an advance praise quote. I was thrilled when I received her report and a copy of the email she sent to Mr. Rash. A few days later she sent me a long critique. I was a new author. Had never participated in a critique group. Did not understand the time and effort it took for her to do this. I was grateful in my thank you note to her, but inside I seethed in reaction to what she suggested. Two or three weeks later, I re-opened the email, read it again. 90 percent of her suggestions ultimately went into the work, and my book is better for it.

On the other side. . .for nearly two years, another author and I wrote from prompts and critiqued our raw work in my living room every Thursday afternoon. She's completely dedicated to writing, and would often have several works going at the same time. Sometimes she read pages from her works in progress for my feedback or ran storylines past me. We worked with respect and honesty, and appreciated each other as people. One day I had to tell her I didn't buy her premise in a nearly completed YA novel, that I knew she could do better. She listened, we discussed it, and then we returned to writing, the subject dropped. I thought everything was fine. Several years later I learned she was so angry with me about the critique, she sat in her car for thirty minutes before she was calm enough to drive home. She'd railed at me to her friends, she said, because I'd unhinged her entire work. She believed me *wrongwrongwrong*. "But when I calmed down, thought about it, I saw you were right," she said. "I rewrote the entire book and my agent loved it."

We want our work loved. We want it to not take so long. To be right and beautiful when we think it's complete. Use critique and rejection to learn from, and get better at being a writer.

Feed your writing life, improve your craft, and support your image of yourself as a writer. Connect with others who understand. There's a list of what others have done at the back of the book for inspiration. All the authors who shared for that list have experienced being stuck, and still do at times. Some things they tried worked to keep them on their feet, feeling centered and strong. And some things didn't work. The key is being open to support and finding what works for you.

Adopt an attitude of inspiration from small everyday triumphs. Understand any sign of recognition is something of value. When querying agents, realize a handwritten two words or lines from an agent is huge. Some get 350+ queries a week! When submitting to journals, rejoice in the editor's request to submit again that comes with the note saying *not this time*. Take it personally in a positive way. You captured their attention with your writing or Voice, if not with that particular story or idea. Maintain the perspective you don't know why you were rejected, and avoid spinning wheels in an attempt to figure the rejection out. It might've been a bad day when the editor read your work and could've been accepted at another time. Look at what you can do differently with your next submission, or consider how you might rework the rejected piece. When you get news you didn't win the contest, but you're a semi-finalist, write it in your evidence journal with a star and exclamation point next to it. You passed the editors' first cuts. They chose to consider you out of dozens, perhaps hundreds. We are more than an One or a Zero, first place winners or losers. Our journeys are measured by more than ones and zeroes. So, see triumphs, not failings.

Garner inspiration from the triumphs of others. Put yourself in their shoes as you read their good news. There's no room or need for jealousy or comparison. You don't know another's struggles or path. Don't know who they know or how long it really took, or what their vulnerabilities are. Connect on social media with a "Congrats" and become one of the tribe of writers there. One day they'll cheer you, too.

I say all this knowing rejection is a blow to the spirit that can feel like a punch to the gut, and it hurts. But you must hold the right perspectives and a large dose of perseverance to not let it get you down. Stay centered in the satisfaction and joy of the process. Keep your eyes on your goals and remember you're a writer despite rejection.

Insulate yourself with intention. Perhaps you enter a cocoon of creating, writing as if no one will read. Perhaps you put rejections aside in a box, and call it a Box of Honor because contrary to being a box of shame or whatever else you may feel at your low point of disappointment, it's evidence you've joined the ranks of greats who got rejections, too. However you insulate yourself, do it in a way that shifts your thinking every time you're engaged so you move forward.

Here's a short list of the ranks you've joined:

- ❖ Stephen King spiked his rejections on a nail over his desk for years before *Carrie* launched his career.
- ❖ Jack Canfield received 133 rejections for *Chicken Soup for the Soul.*
- ❖ Jack London received 600 rejections before selling a single copy.
- ❖ Alex Haley received rejections every week for 4 years.
- ❖ Louis L'amour, popular author of 100 westerns, received 200 rejections before Bantam took a chance.
- ❖ JK Rowling was turned down by 12 publishing houses.
- ❖ Jodi Picoult was rejected by 100 agents.
- ❖ Elizabeth Gilbert treated them like tennis balls, lobbing a new submission back out when she received a rejection.

The authors on this list still living now have first print runs of one million or more. All of them received their rejections before the industry consolidated, when there were more options for publishing through a traditional publishing house, and it still wasn't easy.

Love yourself. Keep writing.

The Inner Critic, A Twisted Friend

The inner critic may deliver the nastiest rejection of all. Its rejection digs in with cruel self-talk in words you'd never say to another person. The inner critic sensors your words, needles you with doubt, and convinces you your work is no good. Seth Godin says the inner critic's rejection is odd behavior that "mostly shows up when others are criticizing us, disappointed or angry about something we did. Odd because it's so useless. In those moments, there are already plenty of other people beating you up. Save yourself the trouble." I believe there are more reasons, and none of them matter because you are a writer doing what writers do, You're a W.I.P., work in progress.

With that said, ignoring the inner critic will get you nowhere because it is trying to help and won't be easily turned away. It's as persistent as any insistent helper can be. Your best tactic is to acknowledge this helper, tell it thanks, then instruct it to sit in the corner *quietly*. Remind it you've got things handled and are making the decisions. (This tactic works wonders with fear, too!)

Perfectionism, The Inner Critic's Buddy

I am a recovering perfectionist. I tend to be on the neat side, believe in doing things right the first time, and don't like answering questions if I can't give an accurate or reasoned response. The only wrinkles in my clothes I forgive are in linen. But perfectionism is complicated and can be an attempt to control, to reign in stimuli, or secure approval and love. All this certainly fits for me. I can track all the reasons. I'm a product of misled intentions, my parents praising me for this malady. My mom confessed she didn't understand me from the time I was very small, so I sought approval in the way I knew got attention—being perfect at what I did. I shared a room with my sister nearly my entire childhood and teen years. My sister a person so completely opposite from me in manner, habits, needs, and her mess that I felt ambushed. I was sensitive and shy, but a talker who loves people and saw the world differently than the average kid or adult. Soon perfection's evil twin, the inner critic, showed up. "Be smaller, less loud. Fit in. Prove you're good enough," it said. It showed up like fear with a mask on.

Nothing stops us moving forward, taking risks, putting out writing out into the world more than a good dose of perfectionism and fear feeding thoughts of not ready or good enough, yet. Even the messiest people who don't give a hoot about wrinkles in their clothes will suffer from fears and shades of perfectionism when it comes to their written work. It puts Velcro on rejection and smothers triumphs. It clouds over what's there and brightens what's not.

"So many of us believe in perfection, which ruins everything else,
because the perfect is not only the enemy of the good;
It's also the enemy of the realistic, the possible, and the fun."
– Rebecca Solnit, author

There is no universal perfection, except perhaps nature and we didn't have a hand in the original creation. What's perfect for one is not necessarily perfect for another. The definition of perfect changes across cultures, societies, and the times. By virtue of being human, you will be brilliant, dull, creative, stuck, good, and bad at any time. And perfectly so, when you are.

Don't settle or stop at good enough every time you work. Don't stop working if you think you'll never be good enough. Live your best creative life. And have fun in the process.

Something easy

Make an altar to your rejections. Whether it's a Box of Honor, a colored folder, a spike, a bulletin board, or a fancy notebook where you keep them. Consider the rejections proof you're doing the work.

What do you fear? What does your inner critic say? What do you see as not good enough? Notice your shades of perfectionism. Write it all down, and say, *I see you. Sit in the corner and be quiet. I have things to do.*

- Pay attention to the evidence journal
- Notice your Yes's
- Schedule and take 10 minute retreats
- Write 5 to 10 minutes from a prompt
- Fill the Evidence Jar with triumphs

Change the Word *Sacrifice* to *Choice*

We make choices every day in our lives. Big choices that define us, and small choices that can define a moment or the rest of our life. When the choices are big they can feel hard, even impossible or unfair. For in every choice we can see a sacrifice. Consider this. . . unless it involves life and death in which you or another are badly hurt, an empowered choice is a triumph. An empowered choice being one made that you decide to make, not one thrust on you. Because you're the one in control, no matter the motivations. You've told fear and anxiety to take a back seat while *you* make the decisions and drive the car of your life.

Easily said, but what about when the choices involve people I love or care about and it's not life or death?

Consider that a choice is a decision that always involves *someone*, whether it's another or yourself. But, oh, that word—*sacrifice*. Visions of arrows and death and pain just thinking the word, right?

Make the empowered choice to hold the vision that everyone benefits when you give yourself time to write. Choosing to appreciate the space and time you have that is less than ideal, your wait for the ideal becomes your only sacrifice. When your writing calls you to sacrifice time with family or friends, you can be more present to them because your soul's not longing for what's missing. Make it an aspiration to have a creative life with writing central in it. Something you build toward.

Six authors I had conversations with specifically used the word *sacrifice*. Five coupled the word with the word *acceptance* and said they made a conscious choice in their trades, which I strongly suspect contributes to a sense of lasting creative freedom on some level in the midst of their busy lives:

A university professor with published works that include a novel and memoir said writing was always a return to her essential self. It had been her lifeline when she sacrificed her own career to marriage and her husband's career. A lifeline that sustained her when she juggled kids, too. She said her faith as a Buddhist helped her release her belief writing was necessary to survive, but it took years. She had to learn to let go of attachment to the outcomes and be in the process (what I spoke about earlier). "I made the sacrifice to be financially uncertain for a period of time to write. I trade financial security for writing time now," she said.

Another author with four published books with the Big Five—three novels (one a NYTimes notable book) and one memoir—made a "lifestyle choice to service her writing." Married now, she said for a long time she deliberately did not couple with a man. When she decided to commit to being an author as her vocation, she also chose manual labor jobs—cleaning houses, packing and moving—which allowed her a life as an author. She had solitude cleaning houses, and the mental space to explore stories and think about the challenges in her writing. While packing, she loved the process of handling belongings, and the stories that went with them the owners shared became fodder for her work. Now she teaches writing and leads critique groups for other writers. And gives back to her writing community with a free writing workshop once a month.

The third is a university-certified ghostwriter and author who loves what she does as a ghostwriter. It uses her best skills, suits her personality, and feeds her interests, she says. But she's never felt fully at peace with the lack of regular financial security that comes with depending on herself to generate paid work, even though the choice was a good trade to her mind because she's living her dream to write and learn. For her, the sacrifice is something to accept and compensate for by being smart in how she's created her life to have time flexibility, choose her own clients, and run her own business on her terms.

The fourth writer shared that he woke Veterans Day knowing he'd follow the voice he heard between his heart and throat that said "Write." He'd heard it a long time, but dismissed it despite wanting creative expression and knowing he had an important story to tell. Degeneration in the school system where he worked that he could no longer tolerate finally pushed him to "commit to the sacrifice." He says the decision was a rational mind choice versus a calling and he hasn't looked back. He's living his dream.

From the outside looking in, the fifth, an award-winning author of short stories and scholarly papers seems to have it made. She feels lucky, she says. She spends time with her two young kids and her husband is her rock that makes everything she juggles work. She's connected to who she is as a person and loves her job teaching at a state college where she has an inspiring, intellectual community on campus. Plus, she loves her community in the town where she lives. And though it hasn't always been so good, her path has been supported by the right teachers, as well as inspired intellectual and spiritual communities focused on the things that matter to her, such as social justice. To top it, she's at no loss for creative ideas. Yet, for all the blessings, she says she writes to stay sane and for balance to the constant navigational decisions of life and family. That there's a constant sacrifice between outside work and creative works. She misses time to read and daydream. Misses space to immerse in her process. But the sacrifices are worth it, she says, because writing is like her "food and water and sunlight."

Each of these authors embraces Writer and Author as central to their identity, not something they do. And the way they could embody that aspect of themselves involved trades and choices. They still feel frustrated, still wish it was different. Still work to change the balance in their lives. But they see the choice as empowering, not defeating. Their choice gives them something that is important to their souls and personhood.

The sixth author has a very different relationship with the trades she may still need to make. She wants space and time to write badly, and feels herself imploding with the desire and need to get down a story she's driven to tell. She set up her office at home to support her writing, and adopted strategies with the kids to carve time. She carries her tablet to work, squeezes writing and research between meetings and her many responsibilities. But she can't bring herself to accept further costs and adjustments in her full family or work life to give her what she wants. "I want it all," she said, knowing her inner peace is the price she pays for not making the trades. I believe she'll write her novel and believe it doesn't have to feel so hard even if she makes no further compromises. Changing the word *sacrifice* to *choice* could create a shift inside her.

Bob Dylan said, "Everything worth doing takes time. You have to write a hundred bad songs before you write one good one. And you have to sacrifice a lot of things that you might not be prepared for. Like it or not, you are in this alone and have to follow your own star."

You don't have to be alone in this. But you do have to follow your own star.

 ### *Two easy things*

Practice thinking and saying the word *Choice* every time the word *Sacrifice* comes to mind or lips. Notice how you feel inside when you do.

Now, complete the following sentence with something positive, either outcome, feeling, or gain: "What if I made this choice to _____?"

It must be a **positive** outcome, feeling, or gain. No catastrophes, losses, or negative thoughts about trades. Meaning, don't ask, "What if it doesn't work?" Ask, "What if this works better than I thought?"

See how you feel inside with your answer.

This is a variation on the Five Minute Journal developed by Intelligent Change (Toronto), adapted here to cheer the triumphs in your evidence journal and support you as a writer.

Complete these sentences. Spend no more than 5 minutes.

1 am grateful for _____

What would make today great is _____

My affirmation for today is _____

One thing I did yesterday I feel good about is _____

I am a writer because _____

- ❀ Pay attention to the evidence journal
- ❀ Notice your Yes's
- ❀ Schedule and take 10 minute retreats
- ❀ Write 5 to 10 minutes from a prompt
- ❀ Fill the Evidence Jar with triumphs
- ❀ Put fears and perfectionism in their place.

KEY #6

You define success.

The word *success* is everywhere. Books are written about it. Attributes of successful people are discussed. We use it to describe businesses, careers, individuals, processes, and products. We have cultural and institutional guidelines for defining success that typically run along the lines of achievement and recognition, or outcomes defined by growth, sales, and financial worth. Reread the passages in the last section about authors who found acceptance with their choices. I read success between the lines: loving one's job that fits who she is; living a dream with purpose without looking back; finding balance integrating work for money and love of writing; feeling lucky, even with the things missed. Few of us have a perfect life in every way, and fewer still feel successful all the time. But what's important is to focus on what success means to you. To know what it is and name it, own it, and embrace it. Realize when the definition is someone else's you may have adopted and that it may be keeping you down.

I'll give you an example of how subjective ideas of success can be. A writing teacher once described me as successful. She viewed my publications, my completed novel, my literary agent, my teaching, my long list of professional retreats and workshops attended as setting me apart. I was shocked she considered me successful because I didn't see myself that way. My goals hadn't been fully realized, yet. The quality of life I desired and how I viewed myself didn't match my ideal or spell success to me. I was shocked at her assessment. It made me seriously consider what success meant for me. Since then, my ideas of success for myself have changed and evolved as my goals, circumstances, and interests evolved and changed. I learned to consider each step forward as having value and each thing she saw as a triumph, even as a win. That said, I admit it's not always easy.

Comparison is deadly.

Comparison can stop us in our tracks. It can throw the most confident or accomplished into a swirl of doubt. It can paralyze and derail us, and postpone dreams. Stop you from taking risks, even good ones like joining a writer's group, going to a writer's conference or retreat, or beginning that book. Comparison is deadly.

You will always find someone or something better or worse than where you are now. No two people have the exact combination of experiences in life, or the exact combination of knowledge, or exact ways of telling their stories. Like two people given the same recipe, the dish will never come out the same. Life is like that, too. You may share the basic details of your life with another, but you'll have different experiences and responses to those experiences. Your lives will look and turn out different.

When you compare yourself, you are in the trap of either seeing yourself as less-than good enough, or as a fraud and impostor. Either way, your full creative potential gets restricted. In the worst case you may even stop writing or never show another person your words. After all, if you're not good enough, why bother? You're wasting your time. Nothing will ever come of anything you do. You certainly won't be seen as a writer, and no class will make you better. On the other hand, if you're a fraud you're fooling people because you are not a 'real' writer. You have no gifts or fresh thoughts and stories. Plus, you may be found out and shamed, embarrassed, or derided. You certainly could never hold your head up as a writer.

The truth is, you are a writer. Where you are NOW, offering what only *you* can offer. You may write for yourself and never share your words, finding that connection in the space between the words for yourself. Or you may share your writing with others, allowing the connections to expand. Even when imperfect, nobody can do *You* like you. There are no comparisons. TV writer and producer Shonda Rhimes says she doesn't believe in the phrase *aspiring writer*. That you're just a writer, so go write. I'm with her all the way on this.

If for any reason you let your writing life whither, you may realize one of two things down the road. One, it didn't matter enough. Or two, you weren't prepared to make it work. Either is okay. But to let it whither because you felt you weren't good enough or you were a fraud is a waste.

Everything in your life feeds the writer in you. Whether frittering time away with seeming inconsequentials, painting the house, taking a walk, eating a delicious strawberry, or creating something of monumental scale, there is no wasted time. Wasted time is a concept against an expectation with an expiration date. There is no expiration date on your thoughts, your feelings, your creativity, or the stories you can write.

So you know even those considered very successful by traditional standards have doubts, consider author Joseph Conrad. He had his wife lock him in a room as he worked on his twelfth novel. Shouted through the door, "Let me out. I never could do this." And Ve Neill, the make-up and special effects artist with a career spanning three decades that includes twenty blockbuster films, eight academy award nominations, and three academy awards who said in a 2016 interview she's never thought she made it. All creative walks at all levels of accomplishment have doubts.

Be clear what success looks like for you. Let go of comparisons. Use them as benchmarks for where you stand today and where you aspire to be or go. The present is the only place where you can start moving forward. Remember, praise only tells us we aren't invisible. We don't need praise to feel success.

"Start from where you are, not where you wish you were.
The work you're doing becomes your path."
-Ram Dass, author

 ## *Something easy*

Define success for yourself. Write it down. Do not censor or judge it grandiose or not enough. This is for you.

Write down what your life looks like when you have success by your terms. Big successes, such as a big dream, and little successes, such as you write five minutes once a week, read five pages in a novel, found five minutes to daydream. Include how you feel when you have those successes.

Observe how you felt as you composed your definition of success. And how it feels when you read what you wrote. Note what emotions come up. How you feel about those emotions.

Now, write down what happens *after* you reach your goals. Be specific, including your feelings.

Take the next right step toward something small or big in your definition of success. Writing a sentence counts.

Put each step taken in your evidence journal with a star beside it.

Share them with someone you trust. Be sure to tell him or her they're your witness. That it's important she holds that space for you without comments or feedback.

Write down how it felt sharing.

Put your sharing in the evidence journal, because you made a declaration when you did that. And a declaration is a powerful thing that should be acknowledged and remembered.

- Pay attention to the evidence journal
- Notice your Yes's
- Schedule and take 10 minute retreats
- Write 5 to 10 minutes from a prompt
- Fill the Evidence Jar with triumphs
- Put fear and perfectionism in their place
- Practice saying the word *Choice*
- Complete your 5 minute journal

KEY #7

We're W.I.P.,
Works in Progress.

Change is the only constant in life. As humans, we grow, evolve, learn, and experience. Good things happen, bad things happen, and every plan changes whether a little or a lot. An old saying goes *the best laid plans of mice and men often go awry*. I like to think rather than going awry, few plans roll out exactly as envisioned. We are works in progress. We falter or fall, and we triumph.

Let me tell you a story. I once created my ideal writer's life. My days completely devoted to writing and authorly pursuits. It took me seven months to clear my commitments in work and to other people for that life. I loved my writer's life, and had it for only seven weeks before I lost it one gorgeous fall morning two weeks after my husband and I returned from a research trip in California for my second novel. He was run down by a car as he walked on a sidewalk. The aftermath of that event swallowed my life from the moment I got the news. He was lucky he survived, but we didn't know if he'd ever walk right again, or how we would pay the mortgage and bills as he was the primary wage earner. I was flung into a black hole of fear and uncertainty, my perfect writer's life stolen and consumed by patient advocacy, insurance companies, lawyers, and caregiving. I woke each morning suffering with severe anxiety, knowing my only way forward was to acknowledge fear, then get on with what I had to do. I wailed, "I want my life back," and in the darkness, I held tight to the one light that didn't flicker—my truth I am a writer.

Merriam-Webster dictionary defines **Author** as one who originates or creates, OR the writer of a literary work. We're all authors writing our stories, in life and on paper. We are all W.I.P., works in progress.

 ### *Something easy*

List all the things you're working on and everything you do as a writer: written works, reading, research, meetings, notes, projects, connecting with other authors, daydreaming, observing with awareness, thinking about your project. Be thorough.

Put a check beside everything on the list that is *exactly* as it was a month ago.

For example:

- ❖ If you were on page three of a story you're writing a month ago, and are still on page three now, a month later, without a single word or comma changed, put a check there.
- ❖ If you were reading a particular book a month ago, and have not read one word or sentence more in the book, put a check there.
- ❖ If you started a story last week or less than thirty days ago, do not put a check there.

❖ If you read one sentence in a novel or wrote a sentence in something you're working on, do not put a check there.

❖ If what you're working on wasn't on your list of writerly things you did a month ago, it does not get a check.

These are simple examples, but my guess is you see few checks on your list. My guess is you've done something as a writer nearly every day.

Note, this is not about intentions, expectations, comparisons, or evaluations. It's about answering the simple questions: Did I do something? Have I moved the needle a fraction in my writing life? And accepting you are a W.I.P.

Whether what I've shared so far is new or you knew it all already, you're beginning to understand that writer's block is about being stuck in some way in your life, aren't you? You realize nothing protects you fully from tripping up or getting stuck along the way, because that's part of being human. The pieces of the inner game foundation outlined here will help you experience lasting creative freedom when you integrate them so well in your cells it's like a voice inside you saying *Get up. You're okay. Watch, keep going. You've got this.*

How you do your life is how you do your writing. Writer's block is linked to what's happening inside and around you, and your response to it all.

Your steps along the way:

● Pay attention to the evidence journal
● Notice your Yes's
● Schedule and take 10 minute retreats

The Writer's Block Myth

- 5-10 min prompted writing
- Fill the Evidence Jar with triumphs
- Put fears and perfectionism in their place.
- Practice saying the word *Choice*
- Complete your 5 minute journal

THE MAGIC WORD THAT WILL SET YOU FREE TO WRITE

There is one word that will set you free to write. The word is Decide. Decide you are a writer and author. Decide what it is you're creating. Decide to value the fifteen minutes you have for writing as much as the hours. The two hours one day a week as good as every day. See every triumph as a drop filling the bucket of your writer's life, like those little pieces of paper fill the jar. View very step as taking you closer to your definition of success. Plan that long breath without distractions. See it, schedule it, and decide to be kind to yourself. Your life is about *Being* first. The race in a life of Doing is a choice, and moves much more smoothly when you include the things that matter to your soul.

Remember, your life is part of your training manual as a writer. Cheryl Strayed says it best:

"... *many people you believe to be rich are not rich. Many people you think have it easy worked hard for what they got. Many people who seem to be gliding right along have suffered and are suffering. Many people who appear to you to be old and stupidly saddled down with kids and cars and houses were once every bit as hip and pompous as you.*"

There are no comparisons.

Every useless day will add up to something the same as every stellar day when you decide and choose to live your best creative life. The bad jobs. The hours writing the words no one will ever see. The long walks and tears. The hours reading stories, poetry, and memories of people you never met. The wondering about every small and big thing. It's all part of the treasure chest of who you are, what you know, and who you're becoming.

So, when you feel squeezed with no time, look to your evidence journal.

When you feel you'll never finish that book, never be validated as a writer, let go of expectations. Experience the process and dance with your creativity where the joy is.

When you long to write, let go of distractions and do what answers Yes inside you. Practice saying No when it aligns with a Yes inside you.

When you feel disconnected and misunderstood as a writer, remember writing is connection. The space between the words a connection with yourself, and a connection between you and others.

When you believe finding the time and space and energy to write costs too much, change the word *sacrifice* to *choice* in your mind and on your lips. Embrace the empowerment a choice made for your soul provides, and feel how much more present you are for yourself and others when you do

When you compare yourself to others, fall into the traps of thinking you're less than good enough or like a fraud, asking yourself, "Who do I think I am?" remember, you define success for yourself and everything's important. The short sentences as much as the completed book. Each step is a triumph. Look at the pieces of paper, your evidence of triumphs, pile up in the jar. Cheer yourself.

When you think you've failed, are not moving fast enough, are not improving fast enough, forgive and love yourself. We are all W.I.P., works in progress.

Every single person is afraid she won't succeed. The PhD is afraid she's not smart enough. The business person is afraid of failing her clients. The bestselling author is afraid she can't top the last one.

You are a writer. An author born to create, to express, to live with your whole being. A person who deserves your best creative life. Decide. And write!

I always imagined I would write a book, if only a small one,
that would carry one away, into a realm that could not be
measured nor even remembered.
~ Patti Smith, author

The Seven Keys
to Set You Free to Write

1. **Pay attention to the Evidence Journal.**
   See what's there versus what's not. Shift focus.

2. **Release control and expectations. Trust the process**
   Open to what shows up versus what you think it ought to be. Dance with creativity.

3. **Let go of distractions. Do what answers YES.**
   Feel yourself expand with the Yes.

4. **See writing as connection. See end products as goals.**
   View each step toward your goals as a triumph, and see triumphs everywhere.

5. **Cheer triumphs. Change the word *sacrifice* to *choice*.**
   Take inspiration from everything you and other writers do

6. **Define success for yourself. Think it. Feel it. Dream it.**
   Remember comparison is deadly. Comparisons are simply benchmarks for where you are now and where you aspire to be.

7. **We're all W.I.P. (Works in Progress)**
   Authors writing our stories in life and on paper.

———❖———

The Magic Word to Creative Freedom—Decide
Decide you are a writer and author. Decide to live your creative life. Decide to value it all.

The Outer Game

7 Greenlights for Success
The Writer's
Permission Slips

The Writer's Block Myth

". . .the remarkable thing about you is your ability to get on
with the job and do your best, despite it all. . .
And you have a choice. More than you might realize."
- Michelle Pizer, Executive Coach, Organizational Psychologist

---

Every morning I step out for a walk. I hesitate a moment, look to the sky, and notice the clouds and how the light changes. I notice colors on trees and flowers and water. Later when I'm out and about, I listen to what people say, consider the stories I hear in the snippets. I try to read a little every day, and often pine for those relaxed hours settling in with a good novel, feeling no guilt over all that needs doing. I'll pine for that sense of immersing in my own work without distractions, too, knowing I've done little pen to paper beyond my blog and poetic Facebook posts. I tell myself I'm just busy, I'm still a writer. Sound familiar?

Sometimes when I'm in the midst of a writing project, I wake to the work and what I need to write next in my head. I think it a good sign. *I'm connected, in it,* I think. But I don't get the perfect thought down before it fades from my mind, which forces me later to try and conjure the exact brilliance I woke to. *This is not good,* I think, and berate the interruptions by my husband and my life because the genius of that thought escaped like a wild bird from a fragile cage. Same in a shower. I'll compose an entire essay as I stand under the spray, run my bath puff over my skin, and forget it with the last droplets wiped from my hair. Even so, at times when I'm lying in bed, lights out and my body exhausted, a link in an essay or line in a poem spins like a runaway tune in my head I can't push away. I jump up, turn the computer back on, and write it directly into the work. In the shower, too. There are times I let the water flow when the characters show up with their stories, and run half-dried to get it on paper. *This* is what a writer's outer game looks like. It's not just putting ink to paper or fingers to keyboard in every moment, and it doesn't always go smoothly. It's embodying everything writers do and giving yourself permission to succeed in the process.

Some people have a negative response to the word *permission*. As a strong woman maturing in a time when women needed a husband's signature to take out a loan to buy a washing machine (yes, that was me), I have an unsettled response to the word *permission*. But we can think of them as hall passes letting us roam free. Go-Aheads and Greenlights we give ourselves. Name them whatever works for you. For now, I'm calling them your permission slips to succeed at the writer's outer game. Because there's no exact science, formula, or process for success that works for everyone. You have to explore and find your own formula without getting bogged down in the process. You have to let creativity dance with your life in the real world and create your writer's life. Poet Mary Oliver said, "The most regretful people on earth are those who felt the call to creative work, who felt their own creative power restive and uprising, and gave it neither power nor time."

These permission slips will inspire and empower you to make your best creative life *your* way, and to own what works for you as the right way. They're designed to take you past stuck and self-doubt when caught in the midst of Life with a capital L. They'll help you with perspective, and solidify the meaning you make of the messages you receive. You'll know that even if you haven't written a sentence in weeks, you're a writer.

Writer You needs no validation. It is a state of mind and identity inside you that can't be successfully split from your life in the 'real' world. A part of you that's always within you, however it looks to others or yourself.

Because your Writer Self takes seriously this crazy wonderful pursuit of putting thoughts into words, words into sentences, into paragraphs, into stories and imparting something that changes and expands a reader's experience in the world in the process. Creating connections with yourself and with others in a way that answers Yes. Your Writer Self may be shuffled, stuffed, and put aside, but it can't be ignored

So, your writer's life needs to be empowered, especially if you feel split, isolated, dismissed, stuck, or otherwise challenged.

Let's get your permission slips now. Your Greenlights for Success.

GREENLIGHT #1

You have permission to do what writers do:
Engage with your imagination & daydream.
Observe with awareness.
Learn your craft.
Research.
Read.
Doodle with words for as long as it takes.

Every one of the activities in the list above equals Writing. Writing is not only pen and pencil to paper, or fingers to laptop. The list may seem obvious, but it's forgotten under layers of expectations, desires, shoulds, and oughts. We often don't give ourselves credit for doing things that seem as much a part of who we are as our writing. The secret, though, is remembering there really is no separation for a writer, except in our heads. Thinking about it this way gives new meaning to the word daydream, doesn't it?

So, I repeat. . . everything in the list—**Engage with your imagination and daydream; Observe with awareness; Learn your craft; Research; Read; Doodle with words for as long as it takes**—equals writing, as well as pen to paper or fingers to keyboard. These activities prime the pump of your writer's life, and are necessary to engage in if one wants to stay on his feet, navigate everyday life, and feel centered and satisfied to write well. Writer's block is life block, after all. And you want your process fed, so move toward your goals.

Each one of these activities takes on different meaning and import, and occupies different space in your life once you embrace writing is a way of being in the world. The things writers do are the foundation of that way of being.

"At its best, the sensation of writing is that of any unmerited grace.
It is handed to you, but only if you look for it. You search, you break
your heart, your back, your brain, and then — and only then —
it is handed to you."
- Annie Dillard, author

Writers engage with their imaginations, and daydream.

Writers let their minds drift until thinking stops. Until pictures, characters, ideas, a question, or story enters. And they wonder about things, allowing curiosity to take them where it leads. Sometimes that wonder leads to a short reflection. Sometimes it leads to an examination of life, or poems, an essay, or a book. Sometimes it leads to the answer to a question, or an unexpected passion like author Elizabeth Gilbert found.

Conversely, some writers let their minds wander until thinking starts. I'm one of those sorts. I wake daydreaming. My early morning daydreams are not an extension of my nighttime dreams, but are an easy glide into whatever drifts through my mind until the tasks and needs of the day or another person intrude. I've called this time before rising my meditation time.

It begins with a character, usually, and once he stands up on his feet and begins to move, all I can do is trot along behind him with a paper and pencil trying to keep up long enough to put down what he says and does."
~ William Faulkner, author

We also engage with our imagination when we let go of expectations while writing. When we follow the characters as William Faulkner and screen-writer-filmmaker Quentin Tarantino do, allowing the unimagined to step forward, or not make sense. We allow space for creativity's full dance.

When you approach writing as a grand discovery or experiment, the process encourages you writer's Voice to emerge. You explore your rhythm and the energy behind how you write best, and make space for the patterns in your way of expression to take hold and mature.

Writers engage with their imaginations while grocery shopping, walking the dog, making the bed, washing the dishes, and playing with kids and friends. Think about how that's true for you. Give yourself permission to be open to your imagination every moment you have.

Giving yourself permission to use your imagination in a story you're drawn to tell can sometimes take a circuitous path. Kim Church, award winning author of the novel *Byrd*, had a character she wanted to know—an independent, capable woman who surrenders her newborn for adoption. Kim searched and found no stories in literature that explored this scenario, so she backed away from the book, feeling she had no authority to write it because she's never had a child. Even so, her curiosity wouldn't let go. She turned to research and interviewed a number of birth parents who had reunited with children they gave up. When she found no universal elemental thread that applied to all of them, she gave herself permission to use her imagination for the character and story.

Every moment spent daydreaming, wondering, pondering, and engaging with your imagination feeds your writing. You are doing what writers do.

Something easy

Take 5 minutes.

Daydream with pen and paper. Write what comes to mind first. Follow the image or character or idea without judging or guiding. See where it leads, and what fleshes out from there, thought into next thought. Release all expectations and intentions, follow the pen without editing or stopping. Let figuring out what you wrote come after you stop writing.

Do not use a keyboard. We'll discuss the reasons why later. For now, write with a pen or pencil.

When you're stuck, remember if something feels *difficult* to do, it links to an intended task or expectation. While something that feels *hard* to do refers to energy spent. Difficult and hard are sometimes part of the process. Know which one you're experiencing so you can identify how to correct yourself back into balance. See triumphs as you move through the hard spots, and cheer yourself.

"Art lets us see the world as beautiful, thrilling, and mysterious."
- David Hockney, artist

Writers observe with awareness.

Read this lovely passage by poet Rachel Ballentine in Albuquerque, NM:

". . . on my walk this morning I saw: the light through baby jackrabbit's ears and the long shadows they cast, pebbles with shadows like minnows, a blue lens on a bridge, a dead tiny yellow bird, a beautiful turquoise door, two large poodles, a datura blooming, the pink suffusion of the sun just before it burst over the sandia [mountains], I heard metal lanyards against flag poles sounding like windchimes, pretty much everyone was still asleep. . ."

There's nothing of what we call 'writerly' in this passage. The beauty is in the simple details and the way she expressed what she observed so you feel the light and the tender small places—long shadows of baby jackrabbit's ears, pebbles with shadows like minnows. You hear things in a new way—windchimes instead of a flag pole clanking. She inserts an image that momentarily stops us with dissonance, the image of a tiny yellow bird, dead. Then she places you with her, sets you in time. Alone, everyone else still asleep. It's early, not bright morning. This is no ordinary description, but a journey she brought you along with simple sensory experience. Her skill lies in her awareness, not simply observation.

I don't know if she spent long on her choices. We can be sure there are many other details she could've included. But I suspect her gaze lingered a second or two longer on the things she shared, and her thoughts hung on the sound of the lanyards on the flagpole a tad longer as she walked. She chose these specific details—color, number, size, state of being, light—because they touched her senses and imagination. Small things that became very special to her that she shared so they touched the reader's senses, as well.

The key is awareness that reaches inside you. What's sparked doesn't have to be a great exploration, but a feeling, thought, memory, or connection you notice. You're affected by the awareness more than the observation. And like Rachel did in her passage, you help the reader feel that awareness, too.

"The world reveals itself when you're on foot."
~ Werner Herzog, author

Everything observed informs our writing. Overheard conversations, behavioral nuances, the changes of seasons and light and color, the mood of the sky or water. You're brought to presence that allows you to expand and be creative. You stretch beyond your current borders. Gain a new pleasure from looking, and observing.

 ### *Something easy*

Sit for 5 minutes. Anywhere is fine—your kitchen, a garden, your office. It doesn't matter. Look around. Notice each thing that captures your attention for even a micro-second beyond your first glance. Color, object, form, shadow, anything. Notice what each of those things that caught your attention evokes inside you.

"Outside the wind is brutal. The sea a sort of brown color, the whitecaps not white but muddy looking. It's supposed to rain today. Even if it doesn't I can't imagine fighting that wind for a walk. But it doesn't matter. I am wondering what it would be like for my character to see the ocean for the first time."
– Nancy Peacock, author

Writers learn their craft.

Simply writing every day does not necessarily make you a better writer. What it does is keep your writer's mind and muscles active, which is indeed important for a writing practice. Writing is like any other thing we do that improves with more skill and practice. But without interest in reading and learning your craft, listening to others' feedback, and studying what makes good writing work, writing alone won't give you the tools to improve.

You *start* by writing. Then you learn how to improve:

You take classes and lessons, go to conferences and seminars, get critiqued. You listen, and read like a writer, meaning you study how other authors do what you want to accomplish. You learn how they tell the story, make transitions, switch point of view, illuminate characters, and incorporate details. You observe how they bring you in and engage you so you suspend judgment, believe them.

You talk to other writers, take note of tips. You get attitude adjustments and realistic perspectives, and apply what we've learned. You practice, because simply writing like we've always written means you write like you've always written.

You understand it may take a thousand words laid down for the one hundred gems. You know that good writing is 10 percent first words on the page, 90 percent revision and editing, and you learn to love that 90 percent. You find the zen in the process, and experience the joy of feeling the work take shape in a more refined way. You know editing and revision are just as creative as writing the first draft because you're still in that space of 'listening and feeling' the work as much as 'doing' the work. You're in the process. You find satisfaction in being the author who's done her best work.

The best gift in learning your craft is it helps get you get past stuck. You have the tools to say what you want to say the way you want to say it. You know which lines you can cross, and how to break the rules. And if you don't, you know where to find advice and answers. Even know how to answer for yourself if a scene or passage works with the whole, or needs to be shot down because it distracts, sidetracks, or confuses the reader. Learning your craft allows you to write the way you intended.

I'll tell you a story. I'm now known for my skill with vivid description. But that wasn't always the case. I taught myself. Remember I told you about the circle of writers I wrote with every week where I received little feedback to what I shared for over a year? I finally asked the right question to carry me forward—how can I reach others with my words? I learned I wrote too densely, with too many layers. The listeners and readers couldn't process what I said fast enough to respond in the time allowed. "Give them something to hold on to," I was told. "Ground them in the world with physical description." From that day on, I practiced description. I learned to tie them to physical experience in the body and give meaning through similes and metaphors. I learned to choose details well enough to select the right dozen out of the seventy pages I read about Appalachian guns for my novel. When my New York agent signed me on, he asked if I was a naturalist. I feared I'd been too descriptive, but he told me that wasn't why he asked. He felt present in the natural world my characters inhabited, he said. A place he'd never been.

I still practice description as part of honing my craft. I compose phrases and sentences in my head to describe what I see when I walk or experience something that feels special to me. I share on Facebook, edit as if they're poetic stanzas. I do what writers do.

 ### *Something easy*

This exercise is for experienced as well as new writers.

When you come up against challenges in your work, don't plug forward. Share with a writer who you trust and can ask what they see that's not working. And read others' work for answers. Ask, *how did this author accomplish what I want to do?*

Go back, reread the passage by Rachel Ballentine. Notice what it is in that passage that helped you see what she saw.

Find one person as a writing partner. A person whose work you respect, and who respects yours. Practice giving critique to each other on your raw writing. It's important you do this with raw writing, as it puts both of you on the same footing and helps limit comparison.

Be sure to focus on what works as much as what doesn't work.

> You'll find some days you feel brilliant, and some days you feel like your mind is nowhere to be found. Which is a great way to get past the things pulling you under as a writer because you're forced to flow with the process, knowing it's all okay. It's rough, by definition!

Writers research.

Author Jodi Picoult says she immerses in the world her book's characters inhabit as research. She follows doctors at hospitals, police on raids, ghost-busters in the field. Author Elmore Leonard gained special permission by judges to spend hours in courtrooms. Elizabeth Gilbert researched the mosses and science that informed her novel, *The Signature of All Things*, for years, traveling to other countries in the process. This sort of research is probably difficult for many of us. But knowing the details of the world you write about, down to the call letters on a radio station, is necessary. A slipped detail can shatter your credibility with a reader. I've been on both sides.

Let me share what I mean. I once put down a novel by a bestselling author because he described spring in Santa Fe as if it was the southeastern United States. Flowers blooming and happy people everywhere. I knew spring in Santa Fe can be very windy and dry. Full of sniffling people suffering with allergies from the piñon trees. I thought the author lazy. He'd put a clichéd image of spring on a place I knew well, and because of that, I didn't think he took the work seriously. Which to me meant the work would not be good. And this was before I was a writer!

On the other side, as an author, the first short story I wrote as a serious writer was set in mid-century rural Appalachia. A culture and place far removed from the big cities I grew up in. One where a negative attitude about outsiders still exists among many. When I decided to follow the story, I had no idea I was writing a novel. Having visited and lived in Asheville, North Carolina for decades, I felt I knew the landscape. But like in Rachel Ballentine's passage, I needed details that would let the reader stand beside the characters and enter their world. Knowing language illuminates a culture's values and reveals patterns of thinking for groups of people, I decided to incorporate it as a tool. Peckerwoods instead of woodpeckers. Poke instead of sack. The double, even triple negatives that capture the rhythm of language and life in the place. Details that were part of everyday lives for the people I wrote about, but showed them unique from other places and times. I also chose details of how they used and interacted with nature, such as making berry baskets from large poplar leaves. When bestselling author Ron Rash who came from generations in Appalachia said that I know the people and place well, I knew I'd met my intention. I use this illustration to underline research is not just about putting characters in a place or lifting information from a book. It's about getting to the place inside you where you connect so well with your material you know what you're writing about. An understanding so evident the reader believes you know more beyond what they're reading. It's one of the ways we write what we know.

Another aspect of research is knowing your expertise and owning it. This applies not only for those who write nonfiction, but for memoirists and fiction writers, as well. Those who write memoirs are experts in the issues at the center of their stories. Fiction writers become experts from research and personal experience. Tom Clancy's heavily researched novels led him to being treated as a go-to expert the media called on during the Iraq war. He didn't tell NBC, 'I'm only a novelist.' He owned his expertise.

Research also applies to knowing your industry if you want to be published.

Whether you seek an agent or query a small publisher for your book, pitch to libraries and bookstore people, or submit your poems and stories to journals, you'll get further and have a better chance of being seen when you understand how the industry works, as well as how to pitch our work succinctly and give them what they want. You'll have realistic expectations, which stops wheels spinning in your mind. Spinning wheels always ensures feeling stuck. You want reasoned responses to rejections, notes on a query, and critique so you write more, submit more, and do the other things writers do so you can take your written works where you desire to go. You did the work.

Writers read.

In author interviews, a question often asked is "What advice do you have for aspiring writers?" 99 percent of the authors respond with one word: Read.

We learn our craft from other authors by paying attention to how they write, even studying what they do. We're stimulated when we read, whether it's a story or treatise. Our feelings are pricked or tickled, and memories awakened. We're prompted to wonder and ask questions that expand our worldview and ways of thinking, and ponder for ourselves how we feel and what we think. We may be shown things we'd never considered, which may lead us down a path we hadn't thought to go before. Our ways of seeing may expand so we see and hear with more awareness when we observe. Ultimately we learn new ways of expression, expand our vocabularies, and hone our abilities to see our own work more clearly. Plus, every time we read, whether for pleasure or information, we're in connection, engaged with something beyond ourselves.

All this informs our writing.

"Read at the level at which you want to write. Reading is the nourishment that feeds the kind of writing you want to do. If what you really love to read is y, it might be hard for you to write x."
– Jennifer Egen

 ## Something easy

Here's a simple and fun way to illuminate your writing now, and how you've evolved as an author.

Make a list of your favorite books, now and in the past.
Make a list of your favorite movies, now and in the past.
Look for commonalities and threads between the two lists.

Genre counts, but you're looking for specifics – themes, time periods, character types, patterns, types of stories, subtexts, endings, etc.

Now, look at what you write.
What commonalities and threads do you see in your writing that coincide with your favorite books and movies?

Share your lists with someone you trust. Ask what commonalities they see across the lists, but don't say what you found first.

When I did this exercise, I primarily wrote fiction. I was not surprised to find flawed outsiders breaking boundaries, a strong sense of place and time, and themes around Home. But I was surprised when a friend noted loss as a central tenet across the board. Something so close to me I completely missed it!

Writers doodle with words for as long as it takes.

Writers write, whether they're published or not. Writers write the fifth or fiftieth draft, and stop only when the work is complete.

Barbara Kingslover admits to sometimes fifty drafts, and thanks her writing group for the seven drafts they read of *Poisonwood Bible*. I heard author Ursula Hegi say she wrote a hundred drafts of the first page of a new novel before she had it right. Ron Rash says he usually writes fifteen drafts of a novel. In an interview for the Paris Review in 1958, Ernest Hemingway is quoted as saying he rewrote the last page of *Farewell to Arms* thirty-nine times before he was satisfied. His response to the interviewer when asked what stumped him, if there was some technical problem—"Getting the words right."

What these authors know, and knew, is they have permission to get it wrong, and to keep getting it wrong until it comes out right. They have the perseverance to let it wobble or flounder under their hand, and not control it. They know, and knew, to settle into the process of living with the story, the characters, intent, and words so that the work can go as far as possible with them and take the form it's going to take. Their first thoughts and intents are the launch of the work, not the limits of the work.

When you're thinking about the end product, let go. Turn yourself back into the process for as long as it takes, even if it takes fifty drafts or ten years. Author Charles Frazier took seven years to complete *Cold Mountain*. Junot Diaz took almost ten years with *The Brief Wondrous Life of Oscar Wao*. He said in an interview for Slate in 2007 that the only success he's had as a writer is by "screwing up over and over." That he'll write a story or a chapter twenty times before he starts approaching what he thinks the story should be. ". . .it is in that process of writing what I'm not supposed to be writing that I find my way to what I am supposed to be writing."

They each have different ways of working, but they doodle with words for as long as it takes.

The Secret Path to Calling Your Written Work DONE

Understanding the process in getting to that point a work is done is crucial. It begins when you reach wholeness in the work. Where all the elements to the story and intent of the work are present. Then, and only then, you progress through completion to that end point when you know it's truly done. Sometimes an author doesn't go through the entire process before the book is printed. These are the books you feel something missing that you can't express. As if the work could've been fuller in a sentient way.

Here's an example. In 2011, author Chloe Rachel Galloway attended a five-day retreat I co-facilitated in which we wrote to prompts every afternoon. She was there to start her memoir, a powerful story of growing up her first twelve years off the grid, isolated in the northern New Mexico wilderness with her family, and the influence her father had on her. Every afternoon when she read I felt a lot of energy around a person in her story she didn't intend to focus on. I suggested she pay attention to what was happening there, despite her intentions. She didn't write her book in those five days as she thought she would, but she found her writer's Voice, and five years later when I offered a four-day Writer's Dream retreat with me as a coach and mentor, Chloe signed up.

She'd written her memoir. Although others told her it was ready to publish, she felt a key element in her story was missing. She could name it in general terms, but couldn't identify exactly how it showed up, or how to approach it. She was stuck, despite the list of scenes she'd outlined to write. And though she understood lots of legitimate things competed with her writing, she felt frustrated it was taking so long to finish the book.

The first day we zeroed in on the missing piece of the story, and how it informed, illuminated, and supported the entirety of the book. It was centered in the person I'd felt so much energy around when she read five years before. This was powerful for her to see and understand, and she credits understanding the path to being done, starting with how the work must be whole before she can move into completing it, as her turning point. It was at that point she saw how all the elements fit together and supported each other, leaving a feeling of wholeness inside her, as well. She wrote 7,000 words over the next three days. The passages she read to me stunning in their completion.

 ### *Something easy*

When you feel impatient, want to be done with what you're writing, or think you should be done, or perhaps even think you are done, get curious.

Pick any page or passage, and ask a *What If* question. For example, if the boy is good, ask what if he's really bad in some way that's not evident, yet. If you're positive what characters are in a scene, ask what if another person showed up.

This exercise is not about the scene or character, but about seeing something in the work you hadn't considered before, even finding something missing. It's a shift in perspective of wholeness and completion.

Have fun with it. Be ready for surprises.

GREENLIGHT #2

You have permission to do it your way. Choose the process that works best for you.

A favorite question for authors that causes people to lean in for the answer is how they write. What's their practice or formula? I'm never sure if it's to show us how similar we are since writing is such a solitary pursuit, or if it's an opportunity to feel a sense of camaraderie. Perhaps there's some hope in the listener that they will glean a tidbit for writing better, or learn something magical that if incorporated, they will be well-read, too. The question is always there, and the reasons people want to know are personal. Just as the process that works for you is personal. One size does not fit all, or even most, and most of us will keep looking for that thing which will make all the difference for our success.

If showing up every day at a certain time works best for you, do it. It may be the only way to get your work done. Make that time sacred. People complete entire books by showing up fifteen minutes every day.

If outlines work best for you, do that. But you don't have to outline. I don't. I combine craft with a huge dose of intuition when I write. I listen and follow the characters as Faulkner did. Feel my way through the story and ideas as I apply my knowledge of craft in developing the plot and structure. My suggestion when you outline is to consider it a guideline versus written in stone. Stories and ideas have lives of their own. It's your job to give them the full light of day in a way that says it best.

Some people work well with deadlines and word counts. I'm not a proponent of that approach. It centers your focus on the end product and a quota versus the time spent, and can take you out of your process. But if that's what motivates and inspires you, and what keeps you moving, do it. It might be the exact tool you need to push you through stuck. Be sure to give yourself permission to move the deadline or word count if the story or your life calls for it. Be aware of the reasons your productivity benchmark changed if you moved it. The reasons are important when setting goals later. You may discover your expectations were unrealistic in the midst of everything you've got going in life, or distractions pull you away, or perhaps it's just plain avoidance. Be aware, and be kind to yourself whatever the reason. I say this from my own experience. I haven't yet beat the thought I'm a failure when I don't meet a deadline. My sign I'm getting better with this is I let go of my thoughts of failure faster. Don't dwell on them as long. Something I call a triumph. (Cheer the triumphs!)

If your best process when writing is linear, do it. But you don't have to. You can write pieces and sections of a work, weave them together. I wrote my first novel as a series of scenes. Sometimes the scenes didn't make sense when I wrote them, such as when a character said it was hot and dusty in a region known as a rainforest. I looked up precipitation records to be sure hot and dusty could be right. Was shocked into trusting my own process after I learned there was a drought the year my story took place. Trust yourself to know your process.

All this applies to how you write, too. Toni Morrison writes her first drafts with a pencil on yellow legal pads and doesn't go to the computer until she's ready to edit. I write first drafts for fiction in spiral notebooks with stiff backs before I move to the laptop. Always in a chair, not at a table. Uniball Jet Stream my pen of choice for years for how it glides and doesn't smear. Author Nancy Peacock writes with a Lamy fountain pen at a desk. Some teachers suggest you write with beautiful tools to help you feel the value in your words. Some suggest you write in nice journals so not only do your words dwell in something special, but you can experience their value when you hold them in a fine volume, and grow brave making mistakes because you sullied a page in a fine book and saw nothing was ruined. My message to you is do what works best to take you closer to your goals as a writer, however it looks, and know you always have permission to make mistakes. It's part of writing.

I have one big suggestion for you in this process. If you compose on a computer, switch to pen or pencil part of the time. I say part of time because I'd be contradicting myself if I said all the time when I'm telling you to find *your* method. I strongly suggest it, though, because something happens in our brains when our bodies are engaged in writing with our hand. Studies show more neural pathways develop, our intuition activates, and we're more creative. If you're not the sort who sees herself as intuitive, think of it as that place where you remember what you forgot. A place where you can slow down, focus on process, not product. Where you let go of expectations. Plus, It's too easy to edit on a keyboard!

Find the rhythm in your writing, whether it's a regular practice or writing in-between the spaces of everyday life. Five minutes a day or two hours a week, or binge writing where you crank out 20,000 words in a few days after not writing for weeks or months.

You can alternate generating new material with editing, or write the whole work and then edit. Work on one project at a time, or on multiple pieces—books, stories, essays, poetry—and move between them. Work with your nature, how you focus for success.

There's a common belief that if you show up to write every day at the same time and write for an allotted amount of time, you will soon adopt a practice. If this works for you, do it. If it doesn't, find your best times to write without distractions when you can feel present and connected. Show up with intention.

Don't be confused I'm saying you only wait for inspiration to write. I believe the time set aside for writing should be sacred time that's protected and honored. Believe intention is everything, discipline important, and practice is key. That a practical approach to your creative work is useful. I also know willpower rarely wins on the long haul. Willpower is the conscious mind against the subconscious mind, and subconscious mind is where motivations and the meaning we make of things that we're unaware of dwell. I'm suggesting you set the intention to find your best rhythm and schedule. Show up with intention to be present, leave expectations at the door, and be open to whatever shows up in the process.

I've often wondered if this scheduled butt in the chair could be a primary source of writer's block for some, and might lead to what author Richard Bausch calls the *season of mists and mellow fruitfulness*. Periods of time when you're working daily without much sense of progress, feeling hyper-aware of failings and that nothing sustains you through your fears and self-doubts. Mellow because it's the time when you tend to go over the work again and again, bored. Mists because you're lost in the process, and are continually thrown back on yourself and your perception of failing.

Here's several systems authors developed and use for themselves:

A speaker and leadership consultant struggled with how to approach writing the book her clients clamored she write. She spent a month actively listening to the questions they asked, reflecting on what they said, and determining what they needed. She then wrote a 'brain dump' of everything she'd tell them and stepped away from what she wrote for 24 to 48 hours. During that one to two days, she kept a private log in which she processed the material without thinking or editing. This system allowed it to take shape before she sent it to her editor to clean up before her final edits on the book. She's now written five books this way.

A former TV writer and school teacher who's now a fiction writer says he never gets writer's block because he constantly feeds himself inspiration. He searches websites and internet daily for ideas and research. Studies a foreign language to help his brain develop neural pathways. Watches four movies a week to open his mind to new perspectives and ways of viewing the world. Whenever he leaves the house or travels, he observes with awareness. He gleans ideas from all his life experiences. He finishes each writing day according to Ernest Hemingway's advice—never empty the well when you stop, leave something to write when you start in the morning.

A highly intuitive author dives into her subconscious when she generates new work. She pictures a glass transparent marble falling into the ocean from a height. She's close beside the marble, falls into the water with it, follows as it descends. As the marble drops, the water grows darker. And when she's deep in her subconscious, she accepts whatever appears without thinking about it and writes down what she receives.

Some authors mind-map. Some do audio recordings and edit from the transcription. Whatever their approach, each author feels confident and creative with their system and writing life.

So, if you don't get the results you want, you have permission to experiment. Perhaps you don't write with an outline, but block ideas. Perhaps you write some parts in a linear fashion, but jump around in the narrative until you have the whole. Perhaps you write the whole work before you edit a word. Whatever helps you move forward, understand your craft, grow as a writer, and feel creative freedom with your process is what you're after. Even if it means daydreaming and observing with awareness for weeks before the next word's written.

Most importantly, work to your nature. Harness your impulses and use your proclivities as empowering tools for your writing. If you work well under deadlines, set goals that will work so you feel accomplishment when you achieve them. If you love trivia, focus on topics that apply to your work. If you're a caregiver, join a writers group where you're part of the collective so you feel your contribution each time you give feedback. If investing money helps you make a commitment and meet it, even when you don't feel like it, pay for a conference, retreat, or writing classes. Think how you can support your own success with the little quirks and buttons you can push in yourself.

 ## *Something easy*

Experiment. Whether you're an experienced writer or just starting to write, sure of how you work or new with no idea what your best system is, think about your life right now. Try different schedules, or different notebooks, journals, and pens. Move around in your home

---

until you find the spots where you like to write most, even if you have a desk already delegated to writing. Pick two places, and alternate time between them. Be creative.

Remember all the things writers do, and consider them triumphs when you engage.

Write the triumphs in your evidence journal. Put a star beside them.

Look through your evidence journal frequently.

If you already write by hand, switch the tool you write with. I just discovered Blackwing pencils, the writing instrument of choice for some of the world's most legendary Grammy, Emmy, Pulitzer, and Academy Award winners. The list includes John Steinbeck, Iris Rainer Dart, Archibald MacLeish, Stephen Sondheim, Truman Capote, Vladimir Nabokov, E. B. White, and Leonard Bernstein. I never thought about a pencil, but the Blackwing is prized for the same reasons I prize my pen.

If you typically compose on a computer, experiment writing with pen or pencil some of the time. Stick with it long enough to get past any niggling attention to the change. Observe and note how what shows up in your writing may be different, and how you feel about those differences. Remember, no judgment. It's all good.

If you feel blocked, let go of expectations. Give yourself permission to do the other things writers do that don't involve pen to paper.

Consider your methods. Write them down so you see what's working and what's not. Try just one new thing for success.

Have fun.

The Value of Pauses

"I came to Weymouth to write and edit and send out query letters, but found I was SO tired and achy, this was about all I could do, besides lots of hot baths and yoga. Now after two days of really paying attention to my body's requests (demands), I find my energy returning, and I am on a roll, folks. Biking tomorrow, along with the writing."
~ Marion O'Malley, author

Pausing now and then is essential to good health for your mind, body, and spirit in life and for your work. You need pauses. Pauses pull you out of the forest so you can see the trees. They're the spaces where you can see your work differently and notice how seemingly unrelated elements might weave into your work.

Pauses are good for the writer's psyche because they give you space to consider and try out how your written work *feels* to you, such as does it feel whole in its concept or execution. They're where you can separate from the task and story at hand, and where you can allow for emotional risk-taking on the page and with yourself.

Poet David Whyte says a pause taken as a 'rest' can be an act of remembering imaginatively, intellectually, physiologically, and physically. An act that brings you to presence in a different way than action does. It's how and where we fall back from goals and targets, and return to process.

Rest is not stasis.

Plus, writing involves a series of decisions, both big and small. It involves intent, word choice, order of words into sentences, into paragraphs, into chapters. It involves punctuation and rules, POV, storyline, message, idea, description, rendering visible to the reader's mind what you imagine, know, and see. Making a connection. Does it make you tired just reading this? Any other endeavor that requires this sort of constant decision-making would deplete you. Your energy would lag and your thoughts become unfocused, as if your brain was melting. Refresh and re-ignite in the pauses. because even if you believe fallow fields should never lie idle, pauses give you a break from expectations. And there are many things writers do to pause and still fulfill that promise of no idle field.

I pause often when I write. I get up, wander to another room. Often it's the kitchen. The question or puzzle I have in the work realigns in my head into a solution during the pauses. When author Neil Gaiman reaches a writing impasse, he puts away his manuscript and ignores it for as long as it takes for his subconscious to take care of the "dirty work," as he says. Stephen King will put a manuscript away for several months before he does his final edits, coming back with new eyes and a new relationship to the work. An author I spoke with said when she reached the last draft of her novel before final edits, she put the manuscript and a stack of critiques from writing colleagues in a drawer for two to three months. She was able to integrate the work with greater clarity when she dived back in with the question, *What is the story I set out to tell?* I, too, try to build in time between edits, even if it's a few days or a week. I'm often surprised how the page and work can look so different when I return to it after a break. I'm always shocked at the number of edits or revisions I do when I thought it complete!

 Something easy

When you feel impatient, ask how you prefer to feel. Switch your focus to how good it would feel the way you want to. For example, when in traffic, you might think *it sure would feel good if I sat here calmly two more seconds*. (To help with that one, consider the average time for a delayed start at a red light is two to three seconds.) With writing, you might think how much you love what you're doing when you're not thinking about anything else and bring yourself back to the present.

Ask what you prefer to feel each time impatience, irritability, awareness, and that impulse to beat yourself up arises.

Step away from the page or keyboard. Do something different to take your brain off-track. Put the challenge you're facing in your work on a back burner. This can take the form of wandering to the kitchen, as I do, or something that demands a complete change of activity such as coloring, hiking, meandering through a museum or shop, or doing the laundry. Don't look for answers to your challenge or think through them. Simply be observant to notice with awareness when they show up.

Change the scenery. Take a new route. Go on retreat.

If you want a different perspective, stand on your head. I'm not sure where I first heard that, but I say it to myself whenever I'm stuck: *Stand on your head, turn the thing upside down. Step out of the box. Look at it differently.*

As a way of standing on my head and finding a different view when I feel the energy in my writing stagnate, I move where I write. I move from desk to dining table. From living room sofa to a chair in a corner of my small office. An author I interviewed doesn't wait until he's stuck. He's designated two places at home as writing spaces, and makes a habit of switching spots regularly. He credits a change of scenery as key to his productivity.

Step out to change the scenery, and mix it up. If you take walks, start from a different direction or try a new path. Turn right instead of left on your standard route. If you typically enter a place through the main entrance, go in through the side or back door. Not only will you see a new view, but you'll notice what you hadn't seen before. Something plain from one side could become fascinating from the other side. Color and light can take on different qualities and intensity. You may hear different sorts of conversations. Your new observations will in turn establish new memories and illicit new emotions.

Our brains rewire to our environments. Author Jules Pretty experienced a striking example of the environment affecting his brain in a physical way. Over the course of a year he walked and explored 400 miles while circumnavigating the shoreline in southeastern England. The sun was always on his right-hand side. When he settled home, he noticed his perception of colors seen with his right eye was bleached with all the blues faded away. His vision in that eye dominated by oranges and yellows "like old film." His left eye still saw saturated colors. Eventually his right eye corrected, but there was no disputing the cause of the change in his sight. He says as writers we must get out and let things happen. Be open and present to everything around us, then bring it home. We must go from "Earthland to Storyland" not as a plod in writing the journey the way the walk was, but sharing the journey inward and outward that occurred while observing on the walk.

There's no better way to step out of our routines and schedules, shed responsibilities of our daily life, and get a new view than to get far enough away so they can't intrude. This is one of the huge benefits of a retreat, whether fifteen minutes, a day, three days, or a week. Not only is the view out the window different, but competition to your writing is removed. Unfortunately, there's a whole list of reasons most people don't take retreats. The three most common reasons being money, time, and perceptions that taking time for oneself is selfish. Followed by fear you won't write as expected.

There's hardly a better way to recharge and get clear than a retreat, though. Remember Marion O'Malley at Weymouth, how much work she thought she'd get done? Instead, her first days were spent resting and rejuvenating, which prepared her to come back to her writing and authorly work stronger and more productive.

A huge benefit of a retreat taken with others is that it gives you a concentrated dose of being around your people—writers!—in a space and place where you can talk about process, craft, and all things writerly. You can be inspired and elevated by what others share, feel understood and heard. You can experience a sense of camaraderie where you bond around your creative passion, and may even feel like a part of a community. So, whether you write chapters or complete an outline or find much needed rest and nurturing, you're supported as a writer and your writer's life is fed.

Since there's always a 'coming back home' from a retreat, be sure to identify and name the specifics of what the retreat meant to you. Identify the most unique and valued aspects of your experience, and what you want more of. Was it space, quiet time, a break from routines, time with other writers, the landscape, solitude? Was it how you felt when there? Or what you did? Think of ways to replicate those feelings, activities, and conditions. How you can carve out solitude, get more nature, have a break from routines. How you can recall how you felt, whether it's through meditation, stories, time once a week with another writer, or touchstones such as a stone or shell or picture you brought back. Most of us can't step away from our lives in the way we may want to at times, but we can know what it is that feeds our creative soul and make plans to have it.

Consider a change of scenery.

 ### *Something easy*

Go out for a long lunch to someplace you're never been before.
Plan frequent walks. Mix it up—direction, time of day, location. Five minutes counts.
Go somewhere you don't usually go, and linger.

Collect a souvenir from a favorite spot or retreat, including mini-retreats. Use it as a touchstone to recall or evoke the mood and feeling that you get from that place.

Try a new, different conversation with yourself around writing:

Tell yourself you deserve a retreat, whether you believe it's a good time now or not.

Ask others you know who have gone on retreats about their experience—how and why they choose the retreat they did; how they paid for it; what they liked about the experience; what they learned.

Look online at writers' retreats. Notice the variety of options from a room of your own to those with organized lessons.

Notice any shifts inside you while you do this. Notice any creative ideas that pop in your mind about what's possible. Can't do a whole week? Consider a day or weekend. Make it long enough for you to shed guilt and habit. Can't do Tuscany? Look to the beach, a place in the country, a place you know you'd love to visit, an Airbnb for a night, or even a friend's while they're away. Ask another writer to go with you. Play with the idea. Notice how you feel dreaming about a writers' getaway.

Time is arbitrary, and on your side.

A soul-killing habit is thinking about what we *should* be doing. It yanks us away from our process and can make us impatient. It can give rise to the impulse to beat ourselves up. Time is on your side. Give yourself permission to be in the process, even to go undercover while you write. The more present you are to process, the more you get done, and the more whole you feel. Which takes you through the process of completion to a finish that is congruent and satisfying. Sounds good just thinking about it, doesn't it?

Something easy

Try this for a variation on prompted writing that includes a pause:

Do a *free write* from prompts.
Put it away for 3 or more days.
Pull it out. Circle phrases, sentences, words, and ideas that stand out or you think are best written.
Take the things you circled and use them as prompts.
Write to the new prompts.

GREENLIGHT #3

You have permission to create and have a writing space.

You have permission to have a space devoted to you and your writing. Whether you create it yourself, or you find a place that feels safe and allows you to write with presence.

It may be a room or a corner of a room, a coffee shop or hotel lobby, the library or a spot outdoors. It may be an alcove or clearing, alone or with others, in silence or with music. It may be an easy chair under a window or a space where you can walk around. There may be shelves with books or a cabinet. It could be half of the dining room table, or a corner of a desk where the documents and papers of life continually pile up no matter how many times you clear them. The point is, know what you need for a creative space—a window, silence, music, a place to sit with your notebook in your lap, or a spot on a table—and create it.

Also know it can change time to time with your mood, circumstances in your life, or creative needs. I used to write at the dining room table or in the living room on my favorite sofa. Then my husband lost his job, was home for months. I moved to a desk in a room where I can close the door.

A room where my writing is shared with the business of our home life. I also had to adjust how I work because when I'm stuck or working through a passage, I like to get up, wander to the kitchen, get a glass of water, make a cup of tea. After five years living together fulltime, my husband finally understood this isn't an invitation to talk to me if I'm writing. I'm still working.

Another example involves an author I coached who'd rented a studio space outside her home. It was quiet and a place she felt nurtured her writing. But over time the building and area around it got busier and noisier, so she considered letting it go. When I spoke with her, she had no place dedicated to writing at home, and she felt challenged not having solitude or psychic space to write. Her desire was a writing shed, but that was not in the near future, she said. As she described her home, the possibilities for where she might carve a place, she mentioned a guest room, describing it as lovely several times. "Perhaps a corner in there," she said. I asked if she had regular visitors. "No, just two or three times a year." I gently reflected she was holding this space empty for twice a year guests, and perhaps this lovely room could be her writing space, given over occasionally for guests versus the other way around.

For years, author Nancy Peacock has kept a small studio apartment separate from her home where she holds classes and hosts her writing groups. She also spends one night a week there to read and write in solitude, eventually expanding that one night to two nights. Her husband understands her taking care of her writer's life needs.

Another author's writing space is a small, dark cubby of an office at home with only two small lights and no external sensory stimuli. She often writes in the middle of the night when the world quiets and her five-year-old son is long asleep.

Any space that works for you is the right space. This is your greenlight and permission to have it. I talk more about this in the next section about creating your writer's life.

It's also important you find a way to let the people in your life know what your writing space is, and if possible, that you reserve it for you and your writing. This is important not just for the space, but because it's an incorporation of writing into your life in a way that validates it to others *and* yourself. Allocating physical space has the effect of elevating perceptions.

If guilt creeps in during this process, tell it to sit in the corner with the other Soul Killers. This space is your portal into your creative life. Where you declare yourself wed with your craft. Women in particular struggle with guilt. The media and societal portrayals of women as nurturers and caretakers of the home and family life are deep-seated. The messages of what a selfless woman is often co-opt ideas of deservedness. These are the kind of messages that say claiming what one wants and needs is selfish when it appears others need or want a piece of us, too. The time and space you take for your writing is your oxygen mask, though. As in an airplane, you must put on your oxygen mask before you help others with theirs.

So you know just how far some will go in finding a writing space that works, consider Junot Diaz. He spent many hours on the edge of the bathtub, the only place he could find to shut out the world to write and edit his Pulitzer Prize winning book, *The Brief Wondrous Life of Oscar Wao*.

 ## *Something easy*

Spend 5 to 10 minutes describing your dream writing space or place, whether you have it now or it's still a wish.

Be specific about how it looks. For example, if it's a gazebo, describe the gazebo—encircled by fruit trees, furnished with a desk, a wall of books, and a red carpet. Include what you see, such as sky from every window, sunshine spreading across the trees and pouring into the room each morning. Red light bathing the room before dusk.

Does your dream writing space have images that inspire? Perhaps relating to the topic or time period you're writing about, as one author has on her wall. Or small pieces of art on your desk as I have? If music is what you listen to while you write, do you have your music close by? Is your desk a favorite color? Author Patti Digh got an orange desk when she created her special writing space. Be specific.

Write down how you feel while in your dream writing space, and why. Be specific about what gives you those feelings. For example, watching sunshine move across the wall gives you a warm, quiet, solid feeling that helps you feel safe and brave to write down anything and everything. Or you feel cocooned, or expansive, or excited to discover what shows up next when you hear certain kinds of music.

Spend an extra moment focusing on the feelings, and what it is that gives you those feelings. Consider how you might create and have those feelings now, with or without that ideal space. Such as you can't have the gazebo with the red carpet and circle of fruit trees, but you can have sunshine moving across the wall, warming you in that special way.

Revisit this often.

GREENLIGHT #4

You have permission to choose what you write.

Sometimes what we want out of our writing dictates what we do as writers. Maybe what you want is a list of publications so you can garner the attention of a traditional publisher. Maybe it's a book so you can stand validated in others' eyes, allowing you to write without explanations. Maybe it's a way to generate income. Or a personal journey that can only happen through telling your story, engaging with memories on the page. Maybe it's to give life to something gnawing your insides—a story, a poem, a desire for expression—that allows you to dance with your love of storytelling. Whether we want a whole volume to hold in our hands, a story to share with the family, or to see our private thoughts in solid form as ink on paper, it all starts with writing the first sentences. The form it takes—short stories, journalistic articles, essays, poetry, memoir, information products, ghostwriting, you name it—will most likely evolve based upon our desired outcomes.

But we don't all sprout as brilliant writers the minute we put words down. We must find our writer's Voice. Learn how to express thoughts, stories, and concepts effectively. Learn how to engage readers. The common adage *writers write*, along with the saying *if you write, you will improve* are only partially true. As I said earlier, writing as you've always written without doing all the other things writers do, including learning craft and knowing how to critique and edit, will not make you a better writer. It will make you a prolific writer.

If you have goals that dictate what form you write, learn how to write that form well. Many writers have an innate leaning where they excel, but it's false most writers can write in any form. For example, if you're a fiction writer, it doesn't necessarily follow that you're good at essays. Or if you write novels that you're automatically good at short stories. Each may have similar craft rules, such as character development, but they have different rules of engagement, such as pacing, how the narrative plays out, and endings.

This doesn't mean a poet or short story writer can't write a novel. Author Ron Rash is skilled writing a variety of forms, and his sensitivities as a poet are not shed in his storytelling. He says in a 2016 Charlotte Observer interview, "Almost everything I write starts with an image. Once I get that first draft down, it's really hearing it. It's the sound. I don't have to read it aloud. I can hear it without that. I become attentive to vowel sounds, stresses—even in the prose. I made 200 changes (between the galley and the finished copy of *The Risen*). Small ones. Where I felt like something wasn't working as far as sound. I usually write 15 drafts of a novel, and the last two are always about sound." The point is, he knows what he's doing in whatever form he writes, and it didn't just happen.

Goals alone are not enough for lasting creative freedom. You won't find an enjoyable challenge or fun experience writing when you're focused only on goals, because writing to goals is a focus on the end result and expectations. Mix passion and interest in and the experience can easily turn to engagement with the process. Let's face it, you can have your sights on the goal, but it's the game and process getting there that holds the fun and encourages you to grow your skills.

For example, I love the process of writing a novel. Settling into the world, following the characters, discovering the themes and conflicts that emerge. I love the challenges inherent in the form, and the complex weaving of threads throughout the journey. I've currently put my novels aside, though, and write essays for my blog because I have goals and feel this is where my work is for now. In fact, I believe this is my best gift to the world right now. With that said, these feelings aren't what keep me showing up to write the blog each week. The weekly deadline I set with an email service to automatically notify readers doesn't keep me in the game, either. Nor the eventual outcome of giving something of value to thousands of readers. It's the adventure I experience each week when I sit down to write. The discovery of what's going on inside me and in my life that I missed while in the midst of it. The sharing of magical moments and my excitement with what I've learned. The fun of weaving stories in the telling. The excitement of ah-ha's I experience at turning points that hinge very similarly as Stephen King's beginnings of stories, with a *what if*. His *what if a car sat abandoned in a ditch in the middle of nowhere?* turns into an alien in a diner. My *what if I thought about this differently?* turns into the thing I need most to move forward. I love that experience of feeling present, more aware and alive, that this process gives me. Even when I'm challenged and it doesn't feel good. Because that ah-ha expands my experience of life and goes beyond my little self. It's part of my interest in psychology, sociology, metaphysics, and the spiritual web of connection in the Universe. Part of my love of stories and poetry. It's also something I can give as well as receive, so it feeds my heart, too. All while it keeps me in the game writing and growing as a writer. It's not the goal, but the experience and process.

Something easy

Take no more than 5 minutes:

What do you enjoy reading?
What do you most enjoy writing? Why?
What are your goals for your writing?
What do you do toward those goals?
What would you like to do more of?
How can you do them?

Put your answers aside. Let them perk inside you.
Add to your answers as more comes to you.

GREENLIGHT #5

You have permission to own your superpower, your writer's Voice.

You have a writer's Voice. It is different than your speaking voice, and different than any other writer's Voice. It is your style, tone, way of expressing, and rhythm in telling and delivering a story or information. It's the way you take readers on a journey.

Find your Voice, and learn to accept it. It's where your genius lies and the one thing you, and you alone, can deliver. It comes from who you are, and reveals your sensibilities, interests, message, themes, and attitudes. It's the non-verbals within the writing. It is your superpower.

Your writer's Voice is the feeling behind your stories and words that readers experience. It's how a reader identifies and connects with you as an author. It's what causes him to say, "Those two words she used, I know exactly what they mean." This recognition, in turn, leaves a reader feeling he knows you as much as he knows your work. When a reader feels he knows you, he'll trust you and travel further and deeper on the journey you take him, and want more. He might even feel you're speaking directly to him.

Consider John Irving, how he always has a writer in his novels. Elizabeth Berg writes intimately about women's inner and outer lives. Frank Herbert created worlds with new languages. Societal moral dilemmas show up consistently in Philip K. Dick's work. We recognize them as much by how they write, what we perceive in their writing, and how we feel when we read their work, as we do by the stories they write.

Develop your writer's Voice and get comfortable with it. One author, a mother and successful blogger and speaker well known in her industry, shared that it took time to find her Voice. She felt self-conscious about judgment, exposure, and being liked. Thought herself a fraud when she first started writing. She wanted to be taken seriously, so she wrote what she thought expected by her business readers, and sounded dry, corporate, with no trace of her personality or sensibilities. Same when she started with social media, she said. Then she put something out on twitter about chocolate pancakes. That tweet had so much response it encouraged her to be more casual. She found her Voice and herself as a writer, and has started a second blog about parenting and work-life balance centered in her desire to share more of her "inspired imperfection," as she puts it.

Your Voice may change over time and across genres. An author who's also a consultant for social media branding believes social media should reflect your life. People who see you online should know your brand, and love you for it. The only way this could occur is through a consistent online Voice. I was long comfortable with my poet's voice and my storytelling novelist's voice. I had to shimmy into finding my online Voice for social media. An authentic voice that reflects who I am with few words. When I started my blog, another personal forum, I had to find my rhythm for essays. And as with author Ron Rash, you'll see aspects of all writing personalities in what I write, including the poet.

When choosing an agent or publications for submission, know where their sensibilities and your writer's Voice fit. For example, an agent who leans toward irreverent humor will not be a good fit for your philosophical novel of ideas, even if he represents fiction. Those who cater to literary fiction may not appreciate your perky beach read. This may seem obvious, but it is one of the peeves agents consistently share. Bottom line, a good fit will lower your rejection rate.

Freelancers are particularly aware of the value in fitting their style and sensibilities to their market. Periodicals and journals can be very specific in their purpose and message. So, a freelancer will often consider a publication's style, tone, intent, and readership before they query with an idea. And may even choose to build their skills geared toward a particular niche within a market they desire for their work. Sometimes developing their Voice for a publication they want to be in.

Ghostwriters are geniuses with Voice. They impart the personality and sensibilities of the people they write for into the work, as well as the words they put down. Their abilities as a chameleon allow them to slip into their own Voice when they write as themselves.

Owning one's writer's Voice can take a tad of courage. Poet Naomi Shihab Nye said, "If you know words, if you compose, you might want to share them because they'll have a bigger life if you do that." A bigger life. What we were reminded of in Part One. . .writing is connection. For her, it seemed more exciting or illuminating to share and see what happened next than to just keep what she wrote to herself. She could not be who she is today, sharing her words to such acclaim, if she had not found her Voice.

I was four years into my writing life before I understood this. And when I did, I claimed my writer's Voice in a declaration on the inside cover of a notebook, dedicating it to the woman who kept me writing in the circle of women that year I wanted to quit every six weeks, Peggy Tabor Millin. This is the dedication I wrote:

I made a decision a few weeks ago. I decide that what I had to say was important enough to learn how to make it heard. That how I said it was good enough. I decided to move forward, risking revelation and rejection—knowing that my Truth may be rejected by some in some places, but will be heard and accepted eventually somewhere else by others.

I have a Voice that is mine and no one else's, no matter how much I may envy them theirs. It is my Voice that I must use and be heard with.

Years after I wrote those words, I participated in an exercise on Voice led by New York Times bestselling author Meg Wolitzer. There were twelve of us in class. Some were in the MFA program at Stony Brook University. Others included an author with a book about to be launched, an editor of a prominent magazine, and a contest winner. We'd listened to and critiqued each other's work, gotten to know the styles of the writers amongst us. On the last day, we received short pieces written by fellow classmates without names on them. Our task was to recognize who wrote each one. A writer's Voice was clear if six or more in class got it right. I confess I passed the test. And I was surprised by some who weren't recognized, including by me who can pick rhythm, tone, and theme, as well as read what's between the lines.

Your writer's Voice is your superpower. Know it. Embrace it. Own it.

 Something easy

Write your own declaration of freedom and dedication to your craft and writing life. Include what you decide to own and celebrate, and your appreciation and acceptance of your writing Voice. If there's someone you want to dedicate the declaration to, include their name.

GREENLIGHT #6

You have Permission to make writing a priority, call it a healthy obsession, and declare it sanctioned solitude.

You have the keys to set you free to write, the foundation of a writer's inner game. You have permissions to use as Greenlights for success. All lead to this one permission to treat writing as a sacred pack with yourself and too make writing a priority, call it a healthy obsession, and declare it sanctioned solitude for yourself.

Every person has an obsession. Some are secret. Some are displayed as collections on shelves and in drawers. Some occur four days a week during football or soccer season. Some show up under a holiday tree, and some are done behind closed doors. Large or small, healthy or unhealthy, whatever the reasons are, each one holds special energy for the person who holds the obsession.

Writing is a healthy obsession.

What writers know that others don't is something happens inside us when we write. We might expand inside, feel more balanced, or have fun with the challenge in a way nothing else gives us. The process of writing can change the way we see ourselves and our way of being in the world. We're more present when we do the many things writers do, and more in relationship to others and life around us. Because when you write, you're making connection with yourself. When you hand what you wrote to a reader and say *this my best, decide what it means for you*, you are making a connection with them.

Whether anyone sees your words or not, being a writer changes you for the better. Even if you should stop writing all together at some point, there's a part of you that is always a writer. It is not the province of special talent or assigned designations, it is who you are.

Our pursuit and desire to write is not frivolous or cute, silly or arbitrary. It is essential.

Jon Bon Jovi says writing *is as close to immortality as you can get*. I agree.

Claim your healthy obsession. Declare you time sanctioned solitude as holy as that of monks in monasteries and caves, and nuns in cloister. Your communion is with the words and dancing with creativity.

 ### *Something easy*

Experiment saying to those who don't understand your need for time to write:

"This is my healthy obsession. This is my sanctioned solitude."

GREENLIGHT #7

You have Permission to succeed by your definition of success.

You have an evidence journal and visible proof in a jar of what's present in your life, and shifted your sights to the space in your life. You've experimented in snippets with trying different things, seeing in new ways, getting clear as you focus on possibilities without judgment, oughts, or shoulds. You know for sure you're a writer, because you do the things writers do. You hold a guide in your hand to remind you how to pull yourself up when you get stuck, and remind you you're not a failure because we all get stuck. Getting stuck is part of being human and Life is just Life. Wildcards even in the calmest of existence, without magic bullets or scripts to count on.

In Part One, the 6th Key to set you free to write is *you define success,* Your 7th Greenlight is you have permission to succeed by your own definitions of success. This is your greenlight to explore that definition, and your greenlight to change it, stretch into it, and stretch beyond it. Or stop when you have it, settle in and see how success feels. Decide if it meets your expectations and satisfies you. Until another benchmark for success calls you to stretch again, and find a new Yes that resonates deep inside you. You're going for YES, and when someone else puts their definition of success on you, an aligned No.

Published, or not. 20,000 books sold, or a single volume in your hand. A book to change the world, or a book to make your family smile. A journal, story, novel, essay, or poem in a notebook, or words scrawled on fine paper. Whatever it is, this is your permission to own it, have it, and know you are okay. Success is how you ultimately feel YES deep in your bones.

 ## *Something easy*

Each night, look into your eyes in the mirror, tell yourself what success looks like for you.

Notice how you feel inside while you say it. Notice how you feel after you say it. Do you feel a Yes, or fear? Empowered, or like a fraud? Guilty, or sure? Like it's possible, or you'll never achieve it and will be a failure?

No judgment of right or wrong, good or bad. Only observation. Whatever you feel is a clue what comes up with you get stuck.

Do it every night.

Note every shift toward a sound Yes in your evidence journal.

A dear friend used to say to my son, *Can't never could. Never try, never will. We're all good.* And when he got older, she added, *What the hell, might as well.*

You're on a journey comprised of shifts and small steps. Your destination is lasting creative freedom.

THE TRUTH ABOUT STORIES

We know stories are how and where we connect with readers. We know they're the basis, even, for the best marketing campaigns. Stories engage us from the time we're small children. The truth about stories for you as a writer, though, is they're your secret permission to succeed because you've been entrusted to tell them, whether from your life or from the ethers.

Author and editor Courtney E. Martin says ownership of our stories and the acceptance of the fact that our stories make us who we are constitutes our relationship with them. They're the most complicated and treacherous part of what we do as writers, because our very Being is linked to them. We can't succeed when that ownership is withheld. When other forces say, *no, that story's not yours, you can't tell it*, they not only killed the story and its place in your soul, they've killed you. What I call the part of you put here to create. Whether it saves you or saves the world, fills in the spaces to make you whole or gives you something to hold in your hand, you're here to live through writing what your creative life means to you.

Write. You have your greenlights and go-aheads to tell your stories and own your writer's life. You have your greenlights to success.

"Look at the mirror every day, appreciate yourself and stop thinking about others that are more successful than you. If you appreciate yourself enough, your success is achievable. Life is like a firework. You gotta ignite the fuse and make it beautiful."
~ Ritu Ghatourey, author

The 7 Greenlights for Success
The Writer's Permission Slips

1. **You have Permission to do what writers do.**
   Engage with your imagination & daydream - Observe with awareness - Learn your craft - Research - Read - Doodle with words for as long as it takes.

2. **You have Permission to do it your way. Choose the process that works for you.**
   To experience the value of pauses and to change the scenery.

3. **You have Permission to create and have a writing space.**
   For you and your writing.

4. **You have Permission to choose what you write.**
   To enjoy the process of your form.

5. **You have Permission to own your Superpower, your writer's Voice.**
   To experiment and develop it, and embrace it.

6. **You have Permission to make writing a priority. To call it a healthy obsession and declare it sanctioned solitude.**

7. **You have Permission to succeed by your own definition.**

The Truth about Stories.
Stories are your greatest permission to succeed.
Because you own your stories. They are a part of you.
They're how you know what writing means to you.

Your Best Creative Life

Living with Lasting Creative Freedom

You have the building blocks of success for creating your best creative life. A guide through the inner and outer games that you can now use as reminders and reference. You have short, easy ways for shifting your mindset to greater clarity, as well as seeing and perceiving visible proof of the spaces and triumphs in your life. Whether you doubt anything's changed for you, or that there are new possibilities in your life now, you know you're a W.I.P., work in progress, which by definition means success for a writer.

You're looking for breath in your life. Looking for the open door to the road you can travel with a feeling of creative freedom as you write, and peace inside as a writer with focus and presence, whether five minutes or two hours.

You understand now that writer's block is about life block. Either something inside you such as unsatisfied desires or expectations, or something outside you such as competition with your writing, lack of acceptance, or shoulds placed on your shoulders. You may have held a yardstick of others' definitions of success to your life, and now can assess what fits and what doesn't because you're working by your own definition of success. You've claimed your superpower, your writer's Voice, and found witnesses who support you. You've moved through acknowledgment to acceptance, and now stand on the threshold of a life of awareness as you claim your last Greenlight, your permission slip to create your writer's life. And if what

I said here doesn't describe where you are right now, no worries. You're a W.I.P.

Lasting Creative Freedom – What is it?

When I asked one author if the thought of lasting creative freedom appealed to her, she replied, "If I have creative freedom, I want it to be lasting." I had to laugh as I thought *of course*. And yet, when I asked other authors, some of them very successful by traditional definitions, they sighed. I could almost hear the desire in their breath. Each author had said *Yes* to my request for an interview-conversation as research for this book. Each took time in their busy schedules. Each said writers need support, and need a guide to help navigate through stuck. They all wanted lasting creative freedom and knew there are no magic wand stores and no magic berries to put under their tongues.

So, what is lasting creative freedom? What does it mean for you?

I can tell you it's not life without bumps or blips or moments feeling stuck. Bumps and blips are part of being human. Lasting creative freedom is available to everyone. It's not only experienced by those with a life filled with authorly pursuits. Your relationship to the page reflects who you are in your writing life. The act of writing and creating forces you into relationship with your thoughts and feelings so you can be guided to recognize how lasting creative freedom feels and re-create the experience.

Creative freedom is an attitude, a feeling, a perspective, an experience that answers Yes. It's a way of being and a belief about yourself that exists between the spaces of every minute and aspect of your life. Even when the minutes and aspects of your life may not look creative on the outside, creative freedom is there inside you, ready to be engaged at any time. Lasting creative freedom is trusting you have a creative life in the midst of stuck.

It does not require you quit your job, your avocations, or give up massive time with family and friends. When it's embodied, it's part of *who* you are. It's an elemental of how you experience the world, and your Being in the world.

Envision Your Best Creative Life

I think all writers want to talk about their writing life and tell their stories. From my experience, people who don't write are fascinated with writers. I often meet folks who know someone who writes. Their eyes brighten with a sort of awe when they speak of their writer friends. Few know how circuitous the route to a writing life can be for an author. The path to that book or blog or commitment in whatever form it manifests, and whether it comes by surprise or was something known deep down in a person from the time she or he was a child.

We often need a bridge between our everyday life of commitments to place, work, and family and our commitment to craft and art and creation. MFA programs, writing groups, and classes can be bridges, but for most of us, we have to create our own.

You know where you are, but what are you bridging to? In this section you'll dream and envision your best creative life. That vision will be the spotlight you follow.

There's no right way or wrong way to create your vision. Food for thought and a guide are important, though, because you want to dig down to the juicy parts of your dreams, which are not always easy to fully know. Either because you're not sure how to get there, or haven't had practice, or are blinded by all the stuff of 'real life' and perhaps buried under others' definitions of success.

Know that the answers to the questions in this section reside in your heart and joy. Writing is not about suffering. It is about Yes. It is not a slow lovely suicide as Oscar Wilde said, but life affirming. The reward for moving through the challenges are gifts of engagement and connection. Doing what writers do is a lifestyle that engages you with presence in relationship to yourself and others, and nurtures your experience of lasting creative freedom.

Deaf percussionist Evelyn Glennis who hears sound with her body says, "Hearing is a form of touch," and the art of listening goes beyond the technical. In music, when you strike a marimba or snare drum, the sound after the strike is an imprint of what happens to sound. I say that's what writers do. We feel the stories with our bodies and in our minds. The connection that happens in the space between the words and ourselves or others is a form of touch. After the words are read (the strike), what happens within the reader occurs. Writing is the way we create our music.

"Instead of a book, what if we're actually writing (or not writing)
in the margins of our lives?
~ Patti Digh, author

LASTING CREATIVE FREEDOM

The short version

Step One – Decide

Decide that no matter what you fear, or hear in your mind, or face from others, or what life hands you, or what you're doing or not doing. . .you are a writer and deserve your writing life. Decide that if you are a writer and it doesn't all feel good, you're getting past stuck and moving forward in the kindest way to yourself and others. You're doing this for You *and* for others. Because you will be happy and that's always good for others. Decide is always the first step.

Remember there are no magic wands to get past stuck, but there is magic in the process. Whatever comes up as you mastermind your creative life, it is EXACTLY the response writers typically experience at this point for changes like this. Meaning, you're fine. You are not a failure or hopeless if things don't slide into place as you thought. Or if you feel doubt, frustration, guilt, fear, or anything else not roses and ice cream. Life is a spiral. We always come back to our issues. The discernment is knowing whether

Heloise Jones

you're going up (looks the same, but not the same) or you're in the same spot (looks the same, is the same). There is no judgment. You simply notice, and decide again.

I have the word Decide lettered on a bright green card in my office where I can't miss it. It's a reminder that gets me moving every time.

Step Two – Choose

Make the choice to acknowledge whatever comes up for you, and accept it's okay. Yep, love yourself best you can. You can even talk to what's in your way. 'Hey, Fear and Loathing, I see you. You can come along, but you're not making the decisions for me.' I've done this many times over many years, including in circumstances that make me cry to think about them. Fear, anxiety, self-doubt, feeling worthless, behind on everything. Bottom line, it works for everything. (Author Elizabeth Gilbert gets credit for the not making decisions part.)

Step Three – Pay Attention to the Evidence Journal

Keep adding to your evidence journal. Pull it out often and look at what you've done versus not done. See the shifts you've already made. Note the time that's there, and how you've added to it.

Focus on the Yes column and let go of Perfection. Believe me, I know this one can be a toughie. But you must. Nothing is as perfect as our ideal, though the layers of how we want to feel inside gets close. How do you want to feel? Go for it.

WHAT YOUR WRITING
MEANS TO YOU

Some writers spend hours on walks in nature and hundreds of pages journaling over years contemplating what their writing means to them. Some come to understand the answer for themselves after diving deep into commitment with a book or blog. Many could answer if they're prompted into the heart of their answer. But you'd be surprised how many writers don't ask themselves the question. This brought me to wonder if perhaps we're offered so many possible answers we might identify with, that considering or exploring the deeper meanings for ourselves in ways that fit our lives doesn't seem necessary.

And yet, we're called to the page and prompted to set goals by what our writing means to us. It is the heart of all we want from our writing and the basis of our agreements with ourselves around writing. The question—what does my writing mean to me?—is not easy to answer in one breath.

Sometimes the answer rests gently in one of two fundamental extremes, details beyond those extremes unnecessary. One, saving your life. Writing carries you through heartache, grief, overwhelming change, and offers escape from demands that threaten to break you. It offers balance and is your life raft, whether as an outlet for creative expression or a place where your heart and soul breathe.

The other extreme, *funktionslust*. The German word for doing something merely for the sake of doing it. It's not about return on investment of time, or getting the gems in the work, or giving us anything in particular beyond the act of creating. Writing's more a scenic route to a destination you're willing to take with no expectations, only experience. Perhaps there's a bit of *funktionslust* in the process of writing for all of us. The thousand words to get those one hundred gems of words because we love it. But I believe if we dive deeper in thinking about this, it's clear the journey is not the same for everyone. So there actually are reasons beyond just doing for the sake of doing.

What I'm optimizing for is freedom, to answer this question. . .
a freedom to spend time honing my craft and then spend time
with the people who matter most to me which are
friends and family."
- Jeff Goins, writer

Here's a few others shared:

- ❖ Writing is my way into self awareness and insight. Processing my life. Perhaps saving my life.
- ❖ Writing's my way to feel absolutely connected to what's in my heart. Something aligned to my passion. That validates me.
- ❖ It's my creative expression, the one that balances what I do in my work and job.
- ❖ Writing's a way to experience the moment I know I created something, did the best I could, and it's good.

- ❖ Words seek me out. A story pushes my insides. I have to write.
- ❖ I have a message. Writing is the vehicle.
- ❖ Writing's part of the bigger picture of my spiritual journey as a physical body.
- ❖ Writing's a gift I have that I can use to do good.
- ❖ Writing makes me feel I'm doing something bigger than a job, because with writing, my job is to open people's eyes and show them something new to think about.
- ❖ I want to touch others in a way that matters, adds to their lives. Writing feels real. It gets me involved in people's vulnerabilities and struggles where the heart and soul of people show.
- ❖ It's my moral responsibility to write and share my experiences for a purpose.
- ❖ Writing starts conversations around things I care about.
- ❖ Writing is a way to connect with my tribe. Those who love the same things I do.

Whatever your reason for writing, know the direction you're headed will change when you're following the work instead of controlling the process. Know that shortcuts rarely exist, and the reasons, even for the extreme answers, lifesaving and *funktionslust,* are varied. I've actually felt both extremes with my writing, that said with the confession I wasn't aware what my writing meant to me at the time.

Then there are the authors who are so clear how fundamentally relevant and necessary writing is to them that they structure their lives to be in service to it, and to allow it to be in service to them.

Author Marjorie Hudson is one such author who's structured her life around writing. She says writing has led her to know her life more deeply. It allows her to connect to her subconscious, live as a literary citizen, and work hard in the collective, giving to and receiving support from other writers. She says writing supports her understanding of human nature and puts her in the world. It allows her to be her whole self with all her gifts and is her connection to the Universe.

In his acceptance speech for the 2008 Nobel Prize for Literature, author Orhan Pamuk stated simply and beautifully why he writes. He presented a list of reasons that included an inability to do the normal work others do, an innate need, liking to read the kinds of books he writes, anger at people, loving the process and the smell of writing materials. He said writing is a means of changing real life, and letting the world know about his country. That literature and the novel are what he believes in more than anything else. Two on his list I imagine apply to many writers—the excitement of turning "all life's beauties and riches into words," and to not be forgotten. His list covered the gambits of selfish and altruistic reasons from the personally sensual to the broad arena of the world.

We can't all do what Marjorie Hudson, Orhan Pamuk, or the other authors who chose teaching and other writing-centric fields as vocations do, but we can be clear about our relationship with writing. We can be clear what it means to us.

Embrace all the aspects of your answer for yourself. This is about you, and you alone. Your answer most likely starts where your story of yourself is centered. A story built over time from experiences, desires, sidetracks, challenges, turning points, and triumphs. One with layers woven like spider threads in a hummingbird nest that become the narrative you've rehearsed and repeated, vivid and true as any memory. You will change as your story changes.

I'll give you an example how connections you hadn't known before can emerge when you start to answer the question. I was once a clay and mixed media artist immersed in the process of the art and challenge of the medium. I loved the immediacy of clay, molding and handbuilding. Loved working with shapes, color, and texture. Loved exploring the cultural and spiritual symbolism associated with many of the materials I used in mixed media. I learned my craft, read, subscribed to industry periodicals, and collected books that filled shelves in my home. I amassed a large collection of beads and elements such as animal parts (bones, feathers), natural treasures (shells, twigs, moss, stones), and figurines. I had my tribe of artists, and attended workshops. Then, somewhere along the line it shifted for me. The rewards no longer held up through life's sidetracks. I still love color and texture, and experience an intimate wonder with those materials I used, but when I found writing I never went back.

Answering the question what writing means for me, I found a connection with what I did as a visual artist. The fine tuning in listening I do when I intuitively write is much like how I engaged with the clay, listening to the material, feeling how far I could stretch it. The combination of rhythm, sound, and meaning in words, sentences, and written images like the combination of textures and meanings in my choice of materials I combined together. I find wholeness in the story like I did when the vision of my mixed media creations came into view. I move through completion as a combination of it all, engaged and present with the process. I love editing as much as the first draft. But unlike any sculpture I created, storytelling and words carry on beyond completion for me. The opportunity to work with words feels more expansive than the physical limitations of hard materials, fire, string, bones. And when I reach what feels like the momentary perfection of a sentence, I'm encouraged forward to the next. The zen is in the craft, knowing there's truly no perfection, but endless possibilities. All a discovery that started with a question, which took me to memory, that brought back to the connections between the two.

Something easy

Consider now what your writing means to you. In the deepest part of your heart and being, the place where you say your prayers and hold your wishes. The place that is yours alone, without worry what others may say.

Answer in a stream of consciousness. Keep the pen moving with a sense of curiosity, open to discovery. Answer it with the full and glorious, or full and simple of it. Flat out truth without thinking it good or bad. Make a list like Orhan Pamuk did.

Be sure to explore your selfish reason, as well as an altruistic reason. The selfish reason is the one all about you. It gives you connection and commitment with yourself. Keeps you going.

You can start with what writing gives you, and what you want to get from it. Why you want to write and do what writers do. What is the reason for your *Why*.

If you need a boost to start, complete this sentence:
I want to write and do what writers do *so that*_____

The altruistic reason, the one about others, gives you connection with yourself *and* connection with others. It gives your writing purpose beyond yourself. Even a short story or novel has the altruistic effect of expanding a readers view, because fiction shows what it is to be human.

So, look at both reasons. Be honest. Look inward, not outward. There are no wrong answers, except the ones that are not true for you.

Like so much else, answering this question is a process with no time limit. Even the authors who believe they know will find more to add to their list. Because the answer grows and changes as you change. It must be considered and embodied over and over again in the course of living. You have to examine if it's become one of the stories of who you are, and why, that you tell yourself based on your history. It could've stopped with a past relationship to this thing called writing, as mine did after those blank sheets of paper I dropped on the professor's desk each Friday when I was 18 years old. The full depth and evolution of your relationship with writing left unexplored.

Social norms are a powerful influence for most of us, too. There's ideas of success and what it looks like added to the pile of shoulds we grow up and live under—what we should do, who should come first, how success should be measured. There's the values we give to those shoulds and the labels that grow out of each one. They all become part of our thinking.

Part One and Part Two are your reminders to fall back on when you stumble or feel stuck, and need help through the snarlies of life. The answer to the big question what your writing means to you keeps you going.

 Something easy

Sit with the question, again. If something comes up and it's hard to admit it, like maybe your answer sounds too grandiose, or on the flip side, selfish, write it down anyway. No one will see this but you. Perhaps your first thought was 'I don't know,' and you let it drop. That's okay, too. Write down your second thought now, and let it perk. Something later will prompt you. That's what happens with us writers.

> Put a piece of paper somewhere you see it. Let the answer continue to roll out as you let the question fall to the back of your mind during your everyday life. Let it rise in your sleep, speak to you when you wake. Write it down.
>
> And when you've answered completely and know you're done, put it aside. After a week, pull it out, ask, "Is this everything? Is this my full answer? What else is there?

Let what you discovered drive your agreements with yourself and help you keep those agreements. Feel the Yes in your chest when you do. I bet that Yes is there. And say often, 'I am a writer.' Even those of you who've been saying you're a writer for a long time, I believe you'll feel it differently this time.

Ask the same question for each of your projects.

What does this book or story or memoir I'm writing mean to me? What do I want from it? How is it linked to my definition of success? How does it tie into my selfish and altruistic reasons for writing.

For example, if your book launch attracts five people who buy a book, is that a success? If it attracts fifty and you don't sell but one book, is it a success? You might consider you also want connection with readers and got it. Or you wanted a way to start a writing group or community as one author shared with me about her launch. She was satisfied, she said, despite small sales. Because she knew what she wanted and she got it. That clarity kept her focused and optimistic and moving forward.

Remember, writing is connection. Connection between writer and the written words. Between reader and writer. To ask what you want from your writing is another level of knowing what that connection means to you. It also supports the adage write *what you know*, because what we know beyond the story that's ours and the research is connecting to other human beings.

It's never too late to create your writer's life.

It's so easy to fall into the trap of thinking too much time's been wasted, or it's too late to live your best creative life. You may think you've invested too much time in a career or job or certain lifestyle to shift how you live to include writing. You may think it's too late to even get started, especially when you see media focused on young authors such as the *30 under 30* lists by the New Yorker, Buzzfeed Books, and the National Book Foundation. But late to writing is no different than late to love, late to a new life, a new career, new friendships, new learning. Developing a craft while choosing to incorporate all the things writers do as part of your lifestyle is about more than holding a product in your hands. It's about the shape of your life and what it means to you.

If I had any doubt what I'm saying here is true, five authors I met in Santa Fe wiped that doubt completely from my mind. The growing season in Northern New Mexico is long, so the farmers market sets up twice a week and extends to the end of November. I was surprised to see a table with a sign that read "Local Authors" one quiet Tuesday. There were five authors, a stack of books in front of each. I met a music composer and former corporate executive who wrote an inspirational book for success based on the wisdom of 19th and 20th century composers. "Not unlike the book you're writing," he said. The others were novelists. One had a sign promoting a series of children's books she was writing. Another displayed three books of very different genres—mystery, western, and contemporary love story. I asked what she liked to write most, each being so different. "I'm 87," she said. "I had fun with them all, hope to sell lots of books. But I'm not writing more." 87 years old! Then I learned the one developing the children's series is in her mid-80s. And a third has been publishing since the 70s, and is still going. They each knew what they wanted to get from their writing life. None thought it too late to start something new.

 ## *Ask the question, again*

Once you've fully embraced what your writing means to you, schedule the next time you'll ask the question. Make a date with yourself and write it on the calendar. Life has a funny way of asking "do you mean it?" when we make commitments to ourselves.

Say your commitments, affirmations, and love songs to yourself out loud while gazing in the mirror. This may be uncomfortable the first few times, but stay with it.

Share with someone you trust who'll understand. It must be someone who understands writing is important to you and that you're a writer, no matter what your day job is. They're your witness only, and need to leave ideas of right, wrong, possible, impossible, and all advice in response to anything you say at the door. And don't ask for advice when you ask for a witness. Save advice for later. If you don't know anyone who can be your witness for this, say it aloud to the sky, or your dog, or your favorite tree. It doesn't matter. Just say it out loud to yourself, and to someone or something in the world.

Don't worry if you feel silly. Remember, the spoken word created the world by some accounts.

YOUR IDEAL WRITER'S LIFE

I think we all have an image of an ideal writer's life. One we believe perfect. We might even think if we could just have that ideal, our frustrations would end. For sure, we'd have plenty of breath and time to get the stories and thoughts down. Dreams are the genesis of a vision, which is the genesis of actions which lead to making our dreams real in the world. Dreams are benchmarks and clarity magnets. They engender aspirations, push you forward in the right direction, and let you know if what you have is enough anywhere along the way because you have the vision, can see where you're going. You can decide if it's worth the cost of the whole ride when you have a vision, too If you achieve your aspirations and still don't feel everything's grand, you know it's something besides the dream that needs adjusting. Dreams are great.

Your dream may include your own small intimate writer's space, like the writing sheds Roald Dahl, Dylan Thomas, and Virginia Woolf had. Or gazebos like Mark Twain's and Neil Gaiman's. It may be a large desk in front of a window with a fabulous view like Diane Keaton's in the movie *Something's Gotta Give*, or a large room with bookcases on one wall like author Chris Bohjalian's. Perhaps it includes a shelf lined with you own volumes, or an extensive library and a comfortable chair by a window for reading.

Heloise Jones

It may include a forum to express yourself, such as a blog or Facebook group, and writer-friends who meet once a week, or an online guided writing group. It could include dream retreats, conferences, and residencies, or working with favorite authors. Your ideal writer's life will most certainly be filled with writing.

An author with four traditionally published books said her image of a writer's life included walks along the river, a desk in a corner, and plenty of time to enjoy her tea. Another said all she wanted was time to write without distractions or outside commitments. They both quit their day jobs at one point, thinking they'd fill it as they'd dreamed. And both returned to work away from home after a year. They got more done with structure to their days, they said. They'd felt guilty while free because writing with pen to paper didn't fill their hours like they thought it should. Now they write more, they say. Both are seasoned writers, know being a writer is more than putting words down, and yet they got stuck, even in their dream scenario. They discovered it didn't work for them as they envisioned.

I had a different experience when I created my ideal writer's life with days completely devoted to writing and authorly pursuits. I loved it. I didn't have a new desk or writing shed, but I had a home to myself and five days a week of solitude while my husband worked out of town. I felt centered and productive, and wrote once a week in my living room with another author. I moved place to place in the house to write when I felt stuck. Wandered to the kitchen, gazed out the windows when I felt challenged on the page. I had no distractions. It took me seven months to clear my commitments for that life. And here's the thing, I had it only seven weeks before my husband was struck down by a car while walking on a sidewalk one gorgeous fall day. Exactly two weeks after we'd returned from a research trip across the country for my second novel. I was spun into a black hole, not knowing if he'd ever walk again or how we would pay the bills. My writer's dream life completely gone in one brief flash. I'm a silver lining gal, even when greeting fear and anxiety each morning, but to find value in the shreds I had to ask what my writing means to me. I needed to know what I still had in those days was enough to keep going until I could rebuild something new. And truth, I'm not entirely there as I write this. Not yet. But I'm not dissatisfied, either. I recognize stuck when I'm in it, and move through. I recognize disconnects happen, and find the triumphs in the tiny spaces and let them hold me up. Some days it's not easy. Some weeks require daily re-evaluations. But I always come back to knowing I'm a writer when I question it.

I share this to illustrate how you can get stuck in your dreams, and the value of re-assessing your dreams. To let the dream image change when it doesn't work to keep you on your feet, moving forward.

Something easy

Have fun with this.

Describe your best creative life. How would it look? Where would you write? What are your favorite places to do the other things writers do—observe with awareness, research, read, daydream and engage with your imagination, or doodle with words for as long as it takes? How would you spend your time? Do you attend conferences, workshops, or writing groups? Go on retreat? How often, how long, where? Do you have a community of writers? Who are they, and how do you engage with them? Include your family and friends, your home, your vacations, and other work. Most importantly. . .how do you feel in your best creative life?

> As always, no editing. No judgment or deciding something too much or impossible. No guilt. No second guessing other people's feelings. Simply dream on paper. Write it as it flows and you imagine it feeling the best. And feel yourself living it.
>
> Now, look at your evidence journal. Are there pieces already present? Are there even small bits of pieces already present? You're on your way.

Let's face it, sometimes it's not enough to piece time in for writing. Writing between tasks can be frustrating, even painful. Rather than give you something to call a triumph, short retreats in a room or corner can feel suffocating and look more like evidence how little you have. I encourage you, though, to open to the possibility that any of those pieces in your evidence journal could expand, grow into your vision in a more satisfying way. If not now, at another time. I fully acknowledge there are no guarantees—this is Life, after all—but it's the possibility you can be open to. The *Yes, maybe*. Even if you say *Yes, maybe in a dream life.*

Your reality originates in your subconscious. The meanings you make of things begin in your subconscious. According to scientists, the only reality your subconscious knows is the one you decide to believe. This is why social scientists have tracked an increase in empathy among those who read novels. As readers experience the emotions, visions, thoughts, and action on the page, it becomes a part of their remembered experience.

Our imagination also resides in the subconscious. Opening with a *Yes* to possibility allows a flow within and around you so your imagination has room to express itself. You'll get a story, a feeling or spark that leads you where you hadn't thought to go. People will show up in seemingly magical ways. Answers to questions, too. I remember once wondering as I walked into a lesson with author Julia Glass how I could move a dog from being a main character in my novel to a background character further along in the narrative. She started talking about her dogs, how there were always dogs in her novels. And I got the answer to my question about the dog in mine.

Say Yes, let yourself go where your vision and imagination lead you.

 ### *Something easy*

Write a love letter to your ideal life. Include your pleasure, your satisfaction, and your happiness feeling the way you do in this creative life of yours.

YOUR PERFECT DAY

I believe most of us could describe our perfect day if given permission to forget we only have 24 hours in a day. Our description of a perfect day would most likely be a combination of past experience and imagined experience. We might even start with remembering one we've had already. When you really think about it, you may discover it's not that every minute of the day was perfect, but at the end of the day you felt good in a most satisfying way. Whether you called it fun, productive, exciting, peaceful, adventurous, stimulating, loving, rewarding, comforting, affirming, or any other feeling that registers as good inside you. You felt it was just right.

No pen, just play with it in your imagination. Play is the key word. Then, pull out the pen, write down your vision of your perfect day.

How does it start?
What do you see?
What's the light like? What kind of light is it?
What sounds do you hear? Close or far off?
Are you alone? Who's nearby or with you?
How does the air feel?
What are you doing? What do you do next, and next?

Where do you eat? What's the place, light, smells, sounds?

Do you sit quietly as you eat?

Is your fiction writer's soul activated so you eavesdrop?

What words and conversations do you hear around you?

How does your writing life, meaning the things writers do, fit in your perfect day?

How do you feel at different times in the day?

What did you like most about the day? What was the most fun? Why? The most satisfying? Why? What surprised you most? Why?

What made you feel the best?

How do you feel overall at the end of the day?

The last three questions about feelings are very important. How you feel, more than what you do, reveals the reason you know the day was perfect. The feelings you experienced are what you want to re-create. This includes how you felt breath and freedom in the spaces, the camaraderie, support, love, friendship, and anything good to your heart and mind. It includes what you feel from the time with other writers, friends, family, or from the pleasure of solitude. The joy of a challenge or satisfaction with an accomplishment count. It might also include all the things your writing and writing life give you. Considering how you feel in your perfect day grounds it in your body.

Consider this. . .some authors shared they want to hold their book in book-form in their hand. When I asked about this, the reasons weren't as much about the printed book or thought of money from the book as it was their feelings. They gave different answers—validation, a sense of accomplishment, a sense of completion in creating something good, satisfaction they contributed to the lives of others, connection with readers. Taking it a step further, a connection with readers who had the same sensibility they did—humor, joy in simple things, and more. Or readers who thought about things the way they did, so understood them. A sort of tribe. All feelings expressed from different people around the central physical act of holding their book in their hand.

We go after things for how they make us feel. We care about getting past stuck because the process of writing gives us something beyond words on the page or a product. We're seeking and wanting lasting creative freedom. We want a feeling of wholeness in which writing fills the spaces of our lives and is the glue that holds us steady as writers no matter what is going on around us.

Jennifer Bourn is known as a blogger, business content leader, and influencer. She thinks of herself as a writer. But when she launched her business with her husband out of their home while pregnant with her second child, she'd never thought writing would be her thing. She wanted to be a teacher when she was younger, and her interests leaned toward graphic design. In 2008, after two years of encouragement, she started a blog focused on business content, and discovered she loved writing. Her blog became her outlet for her own voice and opinions, where she didn't bend her thoughts or herself for anyone else or any other goal. It became a forum for teaching, which she'd always loved. Ultimately, it supported the growth of her business and speaking. She says teaching and speaking *grew out of the writing*. That it is such a core aspect of who she is now that it encompasses her personal brand and how people see her. It's a glue that holds her steady and offers breath in both her personal life and her business success.

As I moved into writing essays I put fiction aside with a promise to myself I'd return to it soon. This was hard. It's been nearly two years as I write this, and I still haven't done that. I feel a loss despite knowing I'll eventually get back into writing fiction, because I know what fiction writing gives me. I know what it means to me.

One is the process. I moved to the computer for nonfiction and don't write with a pen in my spiral notebook. I still feel the poetic rhythm of syllables and words in every sentence. The cadence in the strings of sentences in a paragraph. The breath and intent, too, as I weave stories, images, and other people into the narrative. But I don't 'hear' the work the same, with characters talking and visions behind my eyes which are all exciting and wondrous to me.

The feeling after I finish is very different, too. With fiction, I feel a sense of excitement, even love, when I complete a scene or a work. I fall in love with the characters and story, even the antagonists, and that love sticks with me. Something about stories and people who are beautifully human. On the other hand, when finishing an essay, I feel personal satisfaction, gratitude for the discoveries, and a sense of accomplishment wrangling ideas into making cohesive sense on the page. I'll edit multiple times with the same attention I do fiction and read things later that I think could've gone into the work, but I move on to what's next once the essay's complete. Nothing lingers long afterwards in my heart like it does after writing fiction. I build on what I wrote into my life and other work as an editorial coach, but I don't go back to see if there may yet be another way to immerse more deeply like I do with fictionally created worlds. I consider more what it may mean to a reader and how what I share may add to their lives.

I'm an author either way, but my reasons for writing different forms are different. One very personal, the other both personal and altruistic. The feelings I have afterwards different, but rewarding just the same. Both give me perfect days, but how we want to feel while we write and at end of our perfect day is what we want to create again and again. It is the heart of lasting creative freedom.

OTHER WRITERS, YOU NEED THEM

Your ideal writer's life needs other writers in it. Online, or in a room, coffee shop, cafe, workshop, writing circle. . .anywhere you spend time or find them. Even if you don't know their names, other writers are your support and reality checks, your champions and cheerleaders, your teachers and idea masters. They are your Tribe.

Other writers are perhaps the only people who understand what being a writer is, including the frustrations and joy. They want a writer's life, or at least to write, and have writerly dreams like you. They get what you mean when you're challenged with the story, scene, POV, or process. They have answers to questions about craft, suggestions and advice on perspective, can lift you up when you stumble. They help you persevere rejection and self-doubt. They're the ones whose eyes don't glaze over because they know what you're talking about and understand the exact skill and magic you spin because they're interested. Other writers are your proof it's not just you who feels the way you do. The proof that both the best and the newest at it have shared experiences somewhere along the line.

The Writer's Block Myth

Writing is a solitary pursuit, but that doesn't mean we want to live as an isolated writer. In the end, other writers may be the only ones who don't question what your writing means to you. They know it's important. Writers need other writers.

One author's story says it best. A reader in a family of readers, she knew she wanted to write fiction from the time she was in junior high school. But growing up, she had no exposure to artistic or creative people, and by the time she reached college, she talked herself out of an English major for something practical to appease her parents. She channeled her passion for writing into her journals and themes for screenplays and stories. When her first job with a nonprofit helping teens ended because of a lack of funding, she was bereft. Her former boss offered to pay for a Master's degree. She retraced her steps backwards to her dream and passion for writing, and told him she'd only accept if she could do what she wanted, which was to write. After getting referred to three deans, the head of the department offering the program she wanted informed her that although applications were closed, she'd be considered if she applied with writing samples within a week, at the start of their review. Once in the program, she felt she'd found HER people. Those who understood her desire to create and write, and knew what it meant.

She now has her MFA and a career teaching composition and creative writing. She regularly pushes and inspires fellow writers to invest in their creative lives. She encourages them to submit and participate in the writing community, and believes every writer, outlier on the fringe to the writer of sweet stories, brings something to the table. That we can all help each other not feel marginalized. That we can all help each other with the challenges we face.

Find YOUR people. The ones who understand what it means to write. Create a tribe.

Finding your people

Connect with one, two, or three other writers. Create a support group for your writing life. If possible, meet in person on a regular basis to share triumphs and goals, answer questions get frustrations quieted, and perspectives re-aligned. Put the meetings on the calendar. Give them priority.

I suggest the same time once a week, or every other week. Stick to a time schedule, and keep it constructive. Express your wins, goals, and frustrations. Acknowledge them in others. Then ask what each person needs to walk away feeling empowered moving forward.

If you need ideas how to connect with other writers, look at the Support Guide at the back of the book. Find one or more options that could work for you, and schedule them. It may take a while to establish consistency, but continue until you do. You deserve support.

"Please tell other authors we all need encouragement and a push. That the best thing we can do for fellow authors is look out for each other, network for each other. See this more as a fellowship than a competition. It comes back to benefit all of us in the end."
~ Lenore Harris, author

153

YOUR RITUALS FOR WRITING

How do you enter your writer's mind and space? Many writers have rituals or habits they've established for stepping into their creative mindset. Ways they clear noise in their head or a method of readiness for the internal call of a story or work. Author Toni Morrison says she rises before dawn and makes a cup of coffee while it's still dark—it must be dark, she says—then she drinks the coffee and watches the light come. Light is the signal in the transition, she says. Not being *in* the light, but being there *before it arrives*.

Others read poems or meditate before they begin. Some walk in nature. Many start with a list and go to a prompt, even when they know what they're working on. One author says she maps out her day and sets her intention. That it helps her build writing into her busy life. When she finds herself thinking about what needs to be done, she'll switch to "What do I want?"

Author Ron Rash says he first exercises, then gets a "big half-gallon" of iced tea. Exercise gets him going. The tea gives him something tactile. "With writing, you're inside your head and taking sips of iced tea is taking something tangible. I think that's why so many writers smoke," he says. "Then I get out my pad and sharpen my pencils. There's something about all that that makes the writing easier. It's preparation."

One author I spoke with has two rituals. She once visited the African-American community Jees Bend in Alabama, and picked up a catalog of color block quilts. Before writing she looks at the quilts in the book. Looking at the patterns and colors helps her enter her right brain, she says. And the quilts get her thinking how to piece together words and out of order scenes and episodes. She also reads a poem, which immerses her in language and, like music, can set a rhythm to her thinking.

I have a tendency to walk around with what's up next to write rolling around in my head for hours or days. A sort of semi-meditative state where I'm 'listening' to the story come together. When I know it's time, more a feeling than an intention, I rise before dawn and start, entranced and enfolded. Often I'll stand in the half light before daybreak, drink a glass of water as I hear the words flow through my mind. From that moment onward, I'm able to drop into the work, almost at will.

Do you notice how simple and practical these habits and rituals are? How none involve standing on your head or building in something BIG to do? How most are restive?

Knowing what takes you into your actively creative mind is important, and you can re-create it, even when time is limited. You're working with your subconscious when you activate your rituals. Eliciting a response in your brain that says *we're going into the space with stories, dreaming, listening, connections, ideas, and words now.* The brain becomes conditioned, and once conditioned will move swiftly into that space.

I want to stress that you're working with intention, not expectation. An intention to soften your breath and your mind, open to the process and possibilities of outcomes. Soften into presence, giving your creativity clear space without judgment. This is where creative freedom resides.

Something easy

Consider your rituals and habits for stepping into your creative mind-set. The things that bring you completely into presence with the work.

If you don't believe you have rituals or habits, explore how you feel when you're writing and in *the zone*, what got you there. Is there a pattern of activities you do before you begin working? Do you gather materials, turn off your phone, place a glass of water to the right of your chair? You may be surprised by what you discover.

Practice entering your writing zone at will. And remember, day-dreaming counts.

RE-IMAGINE YOUR CREATIVE LIFE

I read an artist describe how she uplevels her creative life. (uplevel, her word) I immediately thought what she did great for getting past stuck.

She said she challenges herself in a different way each day. She tries different colors, different materials, different styles of drawing. She approaches her work in new ways with the intent she'll create enough information to convey light and shade, the foundation of an image, but not perfection. Only enough to engage recognition within the viewer. She hopes she'll eventually reach a level where she challenges the art world, she said. It's hard to say what challenging the art world means to her, but I can imagine many ways we writers could challenge the literary world. We could start by challenging the concept of who and what a writer is, what a writer does, and what it means to be a writer. Her daily practice is the process I've carried you through in this book with a guide that creates a series of shifts within you so you move forward, see differently, and reimagine your creative life.

Shifts are not about radial change, but upleveling focus, perspectives, and your approach to the page. Upleveling your rhythm doing the things writers do—engaging with your imagination and daydreaming, observing with awareness, learning your craft, researching, reading, doodling with words as long as it takes without judgment or expectations—so that it's part of your way of being in the world, even as you do the laundry, fix lunches for the kids, wait to see the doctor, work at your day job, and juggle the balls life's thrown at you. Upleveling your mind to full presence in the current moments rather that the completed prize at the end, whether it's five minutes or five hours or five days. Being centered in what your writing means to *you* in the midst of the creative life you live. Because all this is what lasting creative freedom is.

You feel validated. You know life's not how often you're stuck or frustrated, or how often you doubt, fall down, question, or feel less than enough. It's about how fast you get up and move forward again.

You trust you're okay, knowing stuck on the page is part of stuck in life, or stuck in one of the writers' mind games. You know you're not alone with this and that this moment is not forever. It is only here, now.

Imagine that.

 ### *Something easy*

If for any reason you're having a hard time with any of these acts of dreaming or upleveling, even one small part of it, use what's called non-dominant handwriting to write yourself through it. The hand you typically write with is your dominant hand, the other is your non-dominant hand. So, if you're right handed, your dominant hand is your right hand and your non-dominant hand is your left hand.

> Start with questions: What's holding me back? What do I need to
> know? or What's here I may be missing?
> Write the question with your dominant hand.
> Answer the question with your non-dominant hand.
>
> It will feel awkward if you're never done it. May even be difficult or
> uncomfortable. But know discomfort can come from different places,
> not just from doing something new like writing with a hand that isn't
> wired to write easily. Your discomfort may come from an emotion
> related to the truth in the answer. So, allow the answers to emerge.
> View them simply as new information to consider and address, or
> not. This is about you and what your writing means to you, and what
> you want.
>
> Use this process any time you're feeling stuck or challenged.

In her book *Upstream, Selected Essays*, poet Mary Oliver says no one has
made a list of places where the extraordinary may happen and may not
happen. That extraordinary's concern is the edge, and making form out of
the formlessness beyond the edge. She's clearly describing the place where
writing occurs.

This is your invitation to re-imagine that space beyond the edge, where
you make form out of the formlessness with words. That's your genius.

CLAIM YOUR DREAMS

One of the questions I asked when conducting research for this book was "What are your biggest dreams for your writing?" The deeper, clearer answer sometimes took gentle coaxing to emerge, and it was often immediate with the right encouragement.

I heard dreams of the author's life—an agent, a big advance, a marketing team, books with beautiful covers and websites for them. Dreams of financial success from writing. Quitting day jobs and long-lived vocations to pursue writing. Having choices in how they create an author's life that supports them. Dreams for outside support to do it.

There were personal dreams—being seen, recognized, and validated as an author. Having time to travel for research and all the things writers do, including time engaged in the process and work, feeling a sense of accomplishment. Having the freedom to choose how they made a living. Some were very personal, with writing tied to their spiritual lives, or their own peace, or a way to show up more vulnerable and honest to others. To live and learn and experience a reward for their Soul by exploring stories.

There were worldly, altruistic dreams—to write novels that are part of a greater literary conversation about our place in the great world. One author used Ta-Nehisi Coates's book, *Between the World and Me*, as an example of such a work. Dreams to encourage support the development of children. Dreams to improve people's lives, expand minds, and elevate the way business is done.

There are dreams for freedom and support—to write whatever and whenever one wants, grow a business through writing, expand one's offerings to others around writing. Dreams to support other writers with a Writers' Resource Center that includes a communal gathering space, private offices, regularly scheduled open mics, libraries, reading and writing areas. Two authors have done work toward establishing resource centers already.

Some shared how their dreams changed as their vision for a writer's life came into view. One author said when she got an agent, her goals grew from writing a good book to include a bestseller that finds readers who love the characters and the world they live in the way she does. Another said part of her dream was moving people on a deeply emotional level with her work.

Some saw writing as fulfilling a mission. One author's social justice mission is to educate people about the plight of gay teens who feel lost, and to prevent the waste of these young lives to suicide. Another feels his job is to open people's eyes, show others new ways to think about things and help create a better world. One wants to inspire others to read. Another to boost the confidence of young girls and help them overcome demeaning societal messages.

You can feel a Yes inside every one of these dreams. Not only do they reflect different definitions of success, but they show how important writing is to people who write. That it's not simply something we do.

Every step in the journey with this guide is to bring you to this place where you claim your dreams and do it *your* way, experiencing lasting creative freedom as you do.

When author Chloe Rachel Galloway was on her Writer's Dream retreat with me, she took a break (one of those important pauses I emphasized) and went to a spa for a hot water soak. Upon return, she told me she berated herself while there for not writing scenes for her memoir as she intended. "And then I remembered what you said about the things writers do," she said. "I decided to observe, and just write without expectation." She shared she often writes short pieces for herself that no one sees, and she wrote one that day. That they're fun to do, and make her feel good. As she read, I knew it was one of the last things I wanted to leave you with. Because this is exactly the feeling I wish you have as you take this guide and live your best creative life. This is what she wrote:

"I am a writer. I'm living the life I've always dreamed of. I'm soaking in an outdoor hot tub, letting my bones rest and my weighted sorrows leave my body. Yes, there are weighted sorrows, even when you are on your path, but you realize there are ways to deal with the sorrows. You realize that love is deeper than you ever imagined. You realize you have the power within to transform. You keep realizing and at times the realizations hurt. You grow deeper and wider and bigger. The tree branches hover over my chair where I sit. I moved from the hot tub to the wooden deck where yellow leaves have fallen. The fall air engulfs my damp skin, while the golden leaves are basking in the afternoon sun. Did I mention I am a writer, did I mention it was my dream to be a writer, to make a living being a writer. I was a kid swinging high from atop tree branches, dreaming big, dreaming of a magical life. This life was far away from me, but what I didn't realize was that I had the very sacred space to dream, the quiet tree line to collect my thoughts, the sunrays to fill my bones, the moonlight to hold my fears. I had it all, but didn't know it, until I learned to write. When I found my voice, there it all was, everything I had been given, everything I needed to know."

CONCLUSION

What does your writing mean to you? Go out, say your answer aloud to someone you trust. Or say it to your dog, the sky, or trees. Hear yourself say it aloud and feel it inside you.

Make an agreement with yourself to live your best creative life. Give yourself your biggest permission slip to claim your dream, create it, and have everything writing means to you.

Remember that permission to meet your agreements will most likely never mean you must forsake everyone and everything else in your life. You know it means you make greater room for YOU in your life, and understand what an unselfish thing this is. Because it means you're living a full life, having more of yourself to give to others. Frustration, unhappiness, guilt, dissatisfaction, and unmet calls from your Soul all contract you, and render you less than who you are across all aspects of your being. Now you can live as fully You with lasting creative freedom.

You know your best creative life is a journey, not a destination. That there will be stops and starts, bumps and resting places along the way. But you know this is the journey you chose, because you know lasting creative freedom defines it and you'll work through your challenges with more clarity and confidence. Your evidence journal and this guide will help you.

The times you get stuck, because it's a fact of life for humans, you'll refer back to the writer's inner and outer games. You'll refresh with the five-to-ten-minute easy things to do that get you moving again, and you'll find help to stay on your feet. The times you're not writing, you'll know you're still a writer because you're doing the other things writers do—engage with your imagination and daydream; observe with awareness; learn your craft; research; read; and doodle with words for as long as it takes.

An accomplished writer I know with multiple books published by Big Five publishers once shared she felt fragile. She's done *all* the things writers do for decades. She has a large network of fellow writers. She knows what her writing means to her and defines herself as an author. Yet she felt she hadn't given herself permission to succeed. What I told her is what I know:

You have permission to succeed. I give it to you. Every single person who's read your words or bought your books have championed you, and gave you permission to succeed. Every word you've written gives you permission to succeed. You're doing the work. Your dear heart, our dear hearts, need to write our own permission slips.

I once heard each of us has an abiding question at the heart of everything we do. That we're always seeking the answer to this question. Mine is, "Am I okay?" Not *safe* okay or *approval* okay, but okay meaning acceptance as I am. Nothing puts me against my abiding question more than my writing does. Again and again it forces me to answer Yes for myself so I can continue my craft, and reach toward that immaculate creation of work and my best self I'll never achieve. And that's why I love writing. My bet is writing answers Yes for you, too.

Go now. Live and love your best creative life.

"...we don't know what day we're on. We just don't. So we've gotta do all we can to make every one be the kind of day that helps us become who we are...sing your own songs in your own voice, in whatever way that means something to you."
~ Tamara Bailie, songwriter

YOUR CREATIVE WRITER'S LIFE WORKSHEET-GUIDE

Thoughts about our writing life can easily become our unexamined stories about ourselves. The full depth and breadth of what writing means to us layered under ideas of right/wrong and possible/impossible with the discovery and evolution of our stories lost.

The answers to these questions are a great review of your writer's life. It's fine if you take time with them. You want a full and honest picture of your creative life.

When done, put your answers away for a month. Make a note on your calendar when you'll look at them again and review what you wrote.

After a month, ask yourself. . . Did anything change? What new decisions have I made? How do I feel about my writing life now?

Revise your answers to include what changed.

Each time you answer these questions brings you more clarity, and you re-commit to your best creative life.

The Writer's Block Myth

From my evidence journal, I see the time I have for writing is _____

I also see _____

The dead-end distractions I can let go are _____

My abiding question, the question that guides my life in all I do is _____

When I think of writing as connection, I think _____

      because _____

I feel successful when _____

Success for me as a writer looks like _____

Besides putting down words, the things writers do are _____

I like to write (novels, short stories, poetry, memoir, essays. . .) _____

      because _____

How I write & create best is _____

When I write with a pen or pencil _____

When I write with a computer _____

My ritual before I write is _____

The way I get present and centered to write _____

When I'm immersed in writing, I feel _____

My ideal space for writing _____

My ideal writer's life _____

My selfish reason for writing is _____

My altruistic reason for writing is _____

What my writing means to me in the deepest part of my heart and being,

without thinking right or wrong, possible or impossible, is

_____

My biggest dream around my writing is _____

Today, I DECIDE _____

READER'S NOTE

As with all guides, *The Writer's Block Myth* is designed to be referred to again and again. So, rest in a chapter along the way. Put it on your desk, your bedside table, bookcase, kitchen counter, or in your bag to use as inspiration and a reminder when you need support or a gentle nudge forward. Experiment and try different things. This journey is about upleveling your creative life.

I wish you all the best.

Sincerely,

Heloise Jones

ACKNOWLEDGEMENTS

A friend once commented, "You love words." At the time I couldn't express how wrong I felt she was. This is what I'd tell her now: As writers and artists we often create in isolation, but relationships and life outside us are what feed our creativity and allow us to write what we know. Writing is not about events, things, or words as much as it is about knowing what it is to be human. Whether fascination with facts, people, or the truly unknowable, we find a place inside us where we can express and share what we know in a way that others can know it, too. I don't love words as much as I love the planet and people, and the connections I see and feel as I write. I don't walk alone.

I wish to thank my husband Art for the space and his willingness to see me through years of creative pursuits. His insights during the times I needed a different perspective made me a better writer, coach, and person.

A Special Thank You to the authors who gave their valuable time and stories, and shared themselves as part of my research:

Robin Jankiewicz
Lenore Harris
Sweetie Berry (http://SweetieBerry.com)
Nancy Peacock (wwwNancyPeacockBooks.com)

Misty Urban (http://MistyUrban.net)

Chris Hale (http://www.ChristineHaleBooks.com)

Bria Burton (http://www.BriaBurton.com)

Kim Church (http://www.KimChurch.com)

J. Patrick Redmond (http://www.JPatrickRedmond.com)

Jennifer Bourn (http://www.BournCreative.com)

Louise Miller (http://LouiseMillerAuthor.tumblr.com)

Fernando Torres (www.FiveTowersPublishing.com)

Bonnie Quick

Elena Mikalsen

Emily Asad

Meridith Elliot Powell (http://www.MeridithElliottPowell.com)

Beth Brand (http://www.BethBrand.com)

Sarah Cook (http://SarahLCook.com)

Kristine Madera (http://KristineMadera.com)

Susan Emshwiller (http://www.SusanEmshwiller.com)

Marjorie Hudson (http://MarjorieHudson.com)

Donna Cutting (http://RedCarpetLearning.com)

Big thanks to author Chloe Rachel Gallaway (http://www.ChloeRachelGallaway.com) for her beautiful reflection that said everything I wanted to say to you at the end of this journey. To poet Rachel Ballantine (http://RachelsBooks.com) for her perfect piece illustrating how observing with awareness and choosing right details helps us connect. And to all the writers who allowed me to use their words, and share my passion for supporting the creative lives of others.

Thanks and appreciations to my publisher Jesse Krieger for his counsel and passion. Passion like his is the best. And to Kristen Wise on the publishing team for her kind words when I stressed and for making the process easy.

Thank you to the writers and artists who said Yes, for their support and affirmations: Nancy Peacock. Chloe Rachel Gallaway, Linda Durham, Ashley Hackshaw, Steve Burdick, Cynthia Lukas, David Witherell, Diane Jones, Wendy Davis, Elizabeth Fletcher, Jacqueline Hill, Kenneth Cameron-Bell, Barrie Trinkle, Shiner Antiorio, and Jesse Krieger.

Finally, thanks and appreciations to you– readers, clients, and friends—for making the world a better place.

I never thought I'd write this book. But when the Universe gives you a charge as it did to me for this book, a work of love can emerge. Sometimes our best offers come from places and things we don't expect.

Heloise Jones

IDEA GUIDE FOR A WRITER'S LIFE

Find Other Writers:

- Critique groups
- Group Retreats
- Residencies
- Conferences
- Workshops
- Writing groups
- Online forums
- Online writing groups
- Social Media
- Workshops
- Partnering with other writers
- Friends to call for craft, support, and anything writerly
- Novel Incubators
- State Writers Associations – local and regional meetings
- Readings
- Writing events

Improve Your Craft:

- Classes
- Teaching (teach to learn)
- Conferences
- Workshops
- Hire an editor
- Hire a coach
- Go to Meet-ups, or start one
- Online
  - classes
  - blogs
  - magazines
  - journals
  - forums
  - workshops
  - webinars
  - info products
  - writing groups
- Engage conversations with other writers about
  - process with other writers
  - skillsets with other writers
  - Engage conversations about being an artist vs. writing for a market
- READ

Ways to set up writing zones:

- Quiet times: on hikes, time before others rise, whenever creative thinking may occur
- Enact a do-not-disturb zone with a sign on the door or your desk.
- Schedule alone times in the house.
- Engage your kids to be monitors for younger siblings.

- Engage your kids in a creative activity of their own with a no talking rule while you write.

Writing Retreats & Residencies

- Arrange mini writing retreats at home with family out for a morning or afternoon.
- Arrange one weekend a month alone, either at home or somewhere close. One author's husband takes the kids and visits his parents one weekend a month. She has 36 uninterrupted hours to write.
- Residencies for published authors through the National Park Service
- Rent a room, house, or condo.
- Author-led retreats
- Check out databases for writing retreats and residencies.

Ask for what you want and need

- Set up a support group

Outside Support

- Grants
- Residencies
- Scholarships (workshops, classes, conferences)
- Internships and volunteer opportunities (conferences)
- Mentoring (often through a community college or writers' association)
- Writing Centers
- *Poets & Writers* and other writers' magazines

THE EDUCATOR'S PACKAGE

For teachers, coaches, mentors, therapists, consultants, writing or reading groups. . .A great supplement for anywhere creativity and/or discussion are key, including workshops, classes, writing groups, conferences, book clubs, consultations and sessions.

- ❖ 30 min. Skype call with Heloise for your group
- ❖ The Creative Life for People Living in the Real World audio training with the core principles in *The Writer's Block Myth*
- ❖ 5 inspirational posters and a Creative Life worksheet-guide to download & print
- ❖ 20 paperback copies for students or clients

www.HeloiseJones.com/educator
USE PROMO CODE *EDU50* FOR $50 OFF

WRITER'S DREAM RETREAT

A private 2-day/ 2-night retreat in beautiful Santa Fe, NM
(other locations available with added cost for expenses)

A dream retreat designed specifically for you that not only supports your process, but accelerates momentum toward your goals.

Leave feeling freed to move forward with your writing and creative life.

<u>Includes:</u>
- **Uninterrupted space & time to write**
- **4 hours of editorial mentoring & coaching**
- **Fine accommodations**
- **Organic breakfast & snacks**
- **The Creative Life for People Living in the Real World audio training with the core principles in *The Writer's Block Myth***
- **5 inspirational posters and a Creative Life worksheet-guide to download & print**
- **Signed paperback copy of *The Writer's Block Myth***
- **10 paperback copies to share**

www.HeloiseJones.com/dream
USE PROMO CODE *WRITE100* FOR $100 OFF